IRELAND
Life and Land in Literature

William A. Dumbleton

STATE UNIVERSITY OF NEW YORK PRESS
Albany

Published by
State University of New York Press, Albany

©1984 State University of New York

All rights reserved

Printed in the United States of America

For information, address State University of New York
Press, State University Plaza, Albany, N.Y., 12246

Library of Congress Cataloging in Publication Data
Dumbleton, William A.
    Ireland, land and life in literature.

    Based on a series of lectures sponsored by the
Capital District Humanities Project and given at the
New York State Museum and Cultural Center in Albany.
    Bibliography: p.
    1. English literature — Irish authors — History and
criticism — Addresses, essays, lectures. 2. Ireland in
literature — Address, essays, lectures. I. Title.
PR8718.D85   1984   820'.9'9415   83-5011
ISBN 0-87395-783-0
ISBN 0-87395-782-2 (pbk.)

10 9 8 7 6 5 4 3 2

IRELAND

For Anna Kennedy and William Dougherty

Contents

Illustrations

Acknowledgments

I AM PRIMARILY indebted to the Capital District Humanities Project in Albany, New York, which sponsored the series of lectures that generated this book. The lectures were given at the New York State Museum and Cultural Center in Albany, and I owe the staff there my appreciation not only for their help in routine and technical matters but more so for the encouraging friendliness that helped to set the atmosphere for the success of the lectures. To the audience of those lectures I owe an especially strong debt. Their dedicated attendance and interest provided inspiration and satisfaction in the preparation of the lectures. I am grateful, too, to Margaret Mirabelli for using her superior editorial skills in changing the spoken lectures to the written word.

I also gratefully acknowledge permission to quote from copyrighted material as follows.

From *Dubliners* by James Joyce. Copyright 1916 by B.W. Huebsch. Definitive text Copyright © 1967 by the Estate of James Joyce. Reprinted by permission of Viking Penguin Inc. From *Portrait of the Artist As a Young Man* by James Joyce. Copyright 1916 by B.W. Huebsch. Copyright renewed 1944 by Nora Joyce. Definitive text Copyright © 1964 by the Estate of James Joyce. Reprinted by permission of Viking Penguin Inc.

From *The Dark* by John McGahern. Reprinted by permission of Faber and Faber Ltd.

From "The Plough and the Stars" by Sean O'Casey. Copyright © 1926 by Sean O'Casey; copyright renewed 1953 by Sean O'Casey. Reprinted with permission of St. Martin's Press.

Introduction

THIS BOOK IS derived from a series of lectures on the Literature and Culture of Ireland sponsored by the Capital District Humanities Project and given at the New York State Museum and Cultural Center in Albany. The book introduces the general reader to the literature of Ireland as it relates to, reveals, reflects, and is an insight into the life of Ireland and its people, as it illuminates their entire culture. Since the discussions which follow grew out of lectures to the public at large, they do not even faintly resemble detailed scholarly analyses of Irish History and its many literary artifacts; nor do they examine all the monuments of Irish literature. Instead they paint an impressionist scene, focusing, where it will serve to bring out the essential pattern, on unusually relevant or exemplary works. Because the situation in northern Ireland presents an enormously complicated residuum of Ireland's historical problems, I have not considered the literature of that conflict. Nor do I pursue the emigrant Irish to their new homes, particularly in America, despite their rich contribution to the literature of their new lands and despite the fact that many of those interested in the material of this book come from precisely that emigrant background.

Since Irish history and Irish politics suffuse Irish literature, the first section of this volume deals with Irish history and the literature that grows from or reflects significant events and those who took part in them. Here we examine some of the difficulties, turmoil, and strife that have been Ireland's lot for centuries, misery which the contemporary literature recreated. Maria Edgeworth's *Castle*

Rackrent, an eighteenth-century novel, depicts the kind of power English landlords wielded over their Irish peasantry. The narrator accomplishes a savage exposé by means of a humor and ironic naiveté typical of the masked hostility of an underclass. The Irish rebellions, particularly that most interesting one, the Rebellion of 1798, generated many fine ballads and songs. So strongly did they rouse the spirit or express the tragedy of an oppressed people that they lived to inspire many later revolutionaries, to say nothing of those who would gather at the pub for a relaxing drink. One horrendous event, the potato famine of the 1840s, preoccupied the Irish imagination in the mid-nineteenth century while obliterating some of that century's stirrings for independence. Though the famine colored most of Irish life during the period, the literature has not traveled to the United States. Perhaps those who fled and their descendants had no desire to rehearse the horror as contemporaries of it portrayed it. One play by William Butler Yeats, *Cathleen ni Houlihan*, epitomizes the Irish situation in the early twentieth century and the role of literature in the movement for Irish independence. Further into the twentieth century, James Plunkett's novel, *Strumpet City*, dramatizes the labor movement in Dublin from 1909 through to the important strike in 1913. Finally, Sean O'Casey's play *The Plough and the Stars* and Yeats's poem "Easter 1916," with their visions of the failed revolution of 1916, complete this sketch of history through literature down to the emergence of the Irish Republic.

Many people feel that there are really two Irelands: there's Dublin and there's everything else. We begin the next section of this book with everything else—country life. The life and values of the Irish countryside differ markedly from, and some feel are more authentically Irish than, the values and life of Dublin. Some of the early romantic and idyllic poems of Yeats, Ireland's greatest poet, convey with warmth and romanticism the Irish country scene, Irish mythological background, and folk superstitions, but its cruel hardships, its realities, come through Synge's play *Riders To The Sea* with tragic clarity. Along with these renderings of country life I have included a short story by Liam O'Flaherty called "Going Into Exile." One of the best works focusing on how families felt when members left Ireland, it properly belongs here because so many nineteenth-century emigrants grew up in the countryside. For centuries, of course, people have left Ireland, but until the improved transportation of the twentieth century, most did so knowing they would never see their families again. It would never tell truth, however, to omit the comic so completely from any discussion of Ireland, and hence we turn to Synge's fine play *The Playboy of the Western World*. Set in a small pub in Mayo, the curtain opens to a world of village life — it touches on father-son relations, marriage and love, and, most tellingly, on coming of age in Ireland.

The next section focuses on the later poems of Yeats. Since Yeats is not only Ireland's greatest poet but probably the twentieth century's greatest poet, and since in his later poems Yeats came to a much more complex and deeper perception of Ireland than he had had in his youth, it befits any survey, however sketchy, to pause and consider these works.

When we turn to city life, to Dublin, we can hire no better guide than James Joyce, with his tales of middle-class Dublin life, *Dubliners*. Among the greatest stories of the twentieth century, they reveal with consummate skill the repressions that Joyce felt shackled the Irish and made their lives dully painful.

Perhaps because only those who attain independence have truly matured, I focus finally on two works about growing up in Ireland. The Irish tend to be rather atavistic anyway, often wanting to turn to the past, so this, as well as the desire for political adulthood, has caused writers to think about childhoods. In *A Portrait of the Artist as a Young Man* James Joyce deals autobiographically with Irish upbringing, Irish schooling, and a very Irish, however personal, search for identity. John McGahern's novel, *The Dark* published in 1965, draws the reader into a more recent Ireland. McGahern and Joyce delineate repressive or restrictive aspects of upbringings in Ireland which both arise out of and have been the cause of many of Ireland's woes. But both books also portray an Ireland which has very nearly, despite the current troubles in northern Ireland, come of age.

This, then describes the broad scene which I hope to show my readers and which will, I also hope, inspire them to further investigation. Each area I so lightly touch on contains worlds for the interested reader — I merely try to make the existence of these worlds known.

1. Handle of the Tara brooch, showing the delicate and skilled interlacing of gold work in complex designs. (National Museum of Ireland)

CHAPTER ONE

The Distant Past

ONE CONCLUSION that emerges from a study of the culture of Ireland is that the Irish, in their literature, look at life from a distinctively Irish point of view. They both see things and respond to them in their own way. Their vision is a dual one which includes not merely the actual but the supernatural as well. They see not only a concrete, physical world but also an imaginative reality that exists in relation to the material reality. Ireland's geographical position and its history isolated this small island from many of the major currents of civilization in Europe until the twentieth century. For instance, although Roman troops were quartered in England from 44 B.C. to 410 A.D., almost four hundred years, Roman forces never inundated Ireland. While they made several forays into Ireland, they never established major settlements. During the four centuries they occupied England, the Romans did not control Ireland.

If you can remember cramming for high school examinations, I am sure at some point you had to list accomplishments of Roman civilization: roads, buildings, and codification of the laws. These hallmarks of Roman civilization emphasize logic, reason, order, and concern for efficient management of a concrete world. Despite the coming of the Germanic tribes, that sense of order, logic, and reason survived and continued to grow with the development of civilization in Europe. What is now called the Western World is a society grounded in the real, the actual, the material, indeed in the commercial. Such materialism remained foreign to the Irish until very recently and exists scarcely at all in Irish culture.

Among those who settled Ireland originally were the Celts. The Celtic people had developed a high civilization, which stretched across Europe, all the way from Greece to Spain, through France, and into the British Isles during a period from about the twelfth to the fifth century B.C. With the Romanization of Europe, the Celtic culture became submerged in all parts of Europe except Ireland, the outer fringes of Scotland, parts of Wales, and Brittany. Thus Ireland remained something of a preserve for this rich culture.

The Celtic civilization had what I will call a primitive imagination, the kind that we associate with most primitive peoples, a highly imaginative view of reality. It was very like the view of reality of the American Indians. If Indians decided that they needed more rain for the corn crop, they performed an elaborate dance to bring about the rain. By putting on a certain kind of costume, and dancing in a particularly prescribed fashion, by stamping their feet a certain number of times, they believed they might, if they performed their dance properly, move the gods to send rain. Notice the physical action of performing that dance. Primitive man assumes that by performing certain physical acts in the material world, he causes certain responses in a supernatural or a spiritual world. The world that the American Indian inhabited was not only a physical realm but a responsive supernatural reality as well. I suggest that the Celtic civilization had that kind of primitive imagination, one that assumed people lived in a reality both natural and supernatural. And while the character of civilization in Europe changed, so that it lost much of that primitive imagination, isolated Ireland retained an imaginative perception that looks at reality with a dual vision.

Irish literature reveals repeatedly that Irish authors want to establish some kind of harmony between the realities of the life they see in front of them and the spiritual realities that they believe or like to believe exist. Sometimes they achieve such a synthesis and other times they do not. This struggle certainly generates much of the tension and energy in the writings of Yeats and Joyce, two of the most significant authors of the twentieth century. And this imaginative vision affects the Irish use of language. The Irish use words differently from Englishmen and from Americans; language is a kind of game. You can't always be sure that what the Irishman says with words is what he means with ideas. When I was living in Ireland, I used to go to get the paper each morning. I would say something obvious on a beautiful sunny day, such as, "Mr. Nugent, it's a beautiful day, isn't it?" And he'd say, "Is this the kind of weather you like in America? I don't take to it myself." I didn't know how to respond at first, and I'd say "Oh," and go. And then on a rainy day I'd say, "What do you think of the weather today, Mr. Nugent?" And he'd say, "It's wonderful, isn't it?" After a while I realized that he was challenging me to a conversation. If he said it was a terrible day when the sun was shining, he didn't really mean that. He was tossing out a little something in language to me which I was supposed to catch and then send something back in return. The two of us remained intact while this little ball of language went back and forth as a kind of game, a sort of pretense. We were not using reality in language at all. What we said was not what we really meant. English novelists in the nineteenth century tended to see their task as one of putting into words the actual reality in front of them. The novels of George Eliot clearly illustrate this. But the Irish very likely would not, because they believed that the realities that they saw in front of them were not all that there was to know. Other things were going on. Thus Irish writers used language more ironically, more satirically, and much much more playfully.

When we look at Irish literature we discover this linguistic playfulness creates a very strong and vibrant thread of comedy. Even in English literature we find that an astonishing quantity of the comedy is actually written by native Irishmen. In the twentieth century, for instance, both Wilde and Shaw were Irish by birth. In Ireland everyone is a comic. I was standing in a small pub in Mayo along with a handful of customers. Although obviously an outsider, I decided to strike up a yet another meteorological conversation. Since it was warm and the sky was a very clear blue, I looked at a man nearby and said, "It's a beautifuly day today, isn't it?" The response I got was, "It's terrible." This time I thought I'd fight back a little. I said, "Well, it does seem to me that the sky is very blue, the sun is out and it's warm and pleasant. I think it is a beautiful day. What do you think is so terrible about it?" He stood silently for a minute and then sputtered, "It's unnatural." I came to grips with that for awhile. "What do you mean, unnatural?," I said. "Well you know, it's not supposed to be this way. And you know what's doin' it don't you?" he mumbled. I said, "Well, in the United States, people would say it's sending rockets into space or testing atomic bombs are doing something or other." and he said, "No, you know what it is, it's the diggin' of the Panama Canal." I remained strong and requested explanation, "I don't understand. Space shots and atomic bombs, changing air currents, I understand, but I don't know about the Panama Canal. It's been a long time since the Panama Canal was dug." And he hauled back and said, "It's the currents of the ocean. If the good Lord wanted the Atlantic to be flowing into the Pacific, He'd have made it that way."

But Celtic imagination, which remained at the root of the Irish nation for centuries, had a richness and quality far beyond playfulness of comedy. The ancient civilization of Ireland gave the country a high cultural heritage. Its was the aesthetic which designed such artifacts as the Book of Kells, the Ardagh chalice, and

2. A close look at a detailed decoration on the Ardagh chalice, showing the elaborate and graceful gold lacing surrounding colorful jewels. (National Museum of Ireland)

the Tara brooch. Their most notable characteristic, the highly ornate interlacings of lines or gold strands, their brilliant color and use of jewels, show a grace and refinement not primitive in the sense of crude or raw.

Aspects of Celtic civilization survived in Ireland through the Dark Ages, helped, in part, by the presence of the Church. What historical evidence we have, and some of it may be questionable, indicates that the Irish were Christianized by somebody we'd prefer to call St. Patrick, who arrived, according to tradition, in 432. (The Anglo-Saxons who had invaded England did not begin to be Christianized until 597 or the early 600s.) The Church assumed responsibility for education, for culture, and it brought with it the advances of civilization throughout Europe at this particular time. The combination of Celtic civilization and the cultural enrichments of the Church in Ireland produced one of the highest forms of civilization in Europe. Some scholars even theorize that when Europe was coming out of the Dark Ages, it turned to Ireland to regain its culture.

The Celtic heritage deserves the high regard the Irish have for it. When most of Ireland achieved independence in the twentieth century, it is understandable that many writers sought to identify the nature of the Irish national spirit, its national soul, by going back, very self-consciously, to Celtic roots. Perhaps, among other things, it helped to overcome the denigration that the Irish bore from the English for so long to prove that there has always been an Irish nation of intelligence, culture, strength, ability, and distinctive character.

One clear manifestation of Ireland's Celtic character is, of course, survival of the Irish language. Even though England dominated Ireland for centuries, not until about 1900 did Ireland finally, for all practical purposes, lose the Irish language. Retention of that language testifies to other Celtic characteristics as well. Only in the twentieth century when Ireland truly became industrial, has it begun to catch up, especially economically, with the rest of Europe. Quite suddenly the Common Market has brought Ireland into association with the commercial world of Europe. And with this comes a dramatic cultural confrontation between the old agrarian value system and a new value system which arises out of a modern society. Today Ireland is once again in cultural turmoil, but a turmoil this time reflecting the changing character of Irish civilization.

CHAPTER TWO

Recurring Enmities

STORY HAS IT that when, in 1014, the Vikings gathered a formidable fleet of ships and headed for Dublin Bay to launch an invasion of Ireland, the elderly Irish king, Brian Boru, knew of the planned attack. He marshalled his army at Clontarf, along the northern coast of the bay. As the invading ships sailed in, the Irish defeated them with their primitive weapons. The Norse turned their boats and sailed away. With a few minor exceptions the battle marked the end of Viking incursions into Ireland.

The significance of Clontarf is clear if you compare this particular attack in 1014 to the Norman attack William the Conqueror launched against England in 1066. He succeeded, and by so doing changed the course of English history and English life. Certainly the English language changed irrevocably. One cannot help but speculate that had Brian Boru failed, and had the Norse indeed overrun Ireland, the course of Irish history would undoubtably have been altered, the Irish language changed, and the distinctive perspective of the Irish lost.

One hundred and fifty years later, however, the contest for power between two Irish warrior kings led one of them, Dermat, to invoke the support of King Henry II of England, who had already developed an interest in Ireland. Forces from England, led by Strongbow, moved into Ireland to begin to assert military and political control. The Irish resisted, and centuries of trouble began. Many of the battle sites of Irish resistance are famous to this day: Castleknock near Dublin and Maynooth in County Kildare along the borders of Dublin. Over the years some of the English settled in

Ireland, often becoming, as the saying goes, more Irish than the Irish themselves. (This still happens to some Americans who travel to Ireland when they take on a strong brogue and become more Irish than the Irish themselves.) In effect the twelfth-century invaders never really conquered Ireland. They were either resisted by the Irish or were absorbed by them. But the English continued to try, and English monarchs, when confronted at home with military or political troublemakers, usually sent them to Ireland in hopes they would work out their ambitions there.

During one English-Irish skirmish a famous Irish family, the Fitzgeralds, led the resistance. After much action the two sides finally made a treaty according to which the antagonistic parties would separate and draw a line. The English would gain a prescribed amount of territory within which English law and custom would rule. That line, called the Pale, enclosed an area about twenty miles in radius, surrounding Dublin. The popular expression still heard — that something is beyond the Pale — results from that particular line. The line of the Pale went through the Town of Maynooth on the outskirts of Dublin and it's there that over the years the Geraldine families built their big houses. The Geraldine family's Carton House still stands as a notable attraction for tourists.

The Irish resistance to English incursions continued into the reign of the Tudor kings. When the Tudor Henry VIII broke with the Church of Rome, English-Irish differences intensified, for the Irish people and the Irish clergy remained loyal to Rome. This sharpened the political difficulties between the Irish, who remained Catholic, and the English who were now Protestant. Why the Irish felt so strongly loyal to the Church of Rome while the English did not is a speculation of history. But the Irish did, with great tenacity, hold to Rome. According to King Henry VIII, however, to refuse the Church of England, which he now headed, was to commit a treasonous act as well as a heretical one.

Ireland's loyalty to Rome had strategic consequences. Catholic Spain, England's principal adversary, could find sympathetic aid from Catholic Ireland. This was no idle threat since Ireland lay so close to England. Although Elizabeth I's defeat of the Spanish Armada in 1588 ended that era's immediate threat to England, the nearness of Ireland to England remained a significant problem for England up to and including World War II.

Fearing Spain might find Catholic sympathies in Ireland, the

Tudors hoped to subdue Ireland at last, to punish the Irish for any resistance and to confiscate the land. The Irish fought back, of course, but the invading armies prevailed. Among the many Irish heroes of this time we find was another Fitzgerald from Maynooth, a man with the intriguing name of Sillen Thomas Fitzgerald, and one Hugh O'Neill, from County Tyrone. The Irish-American playwright Eugene O'Neill named the family in his outstanding autobiographical play, *A Long Day's Journey Into Night*, Tyrone and he uses the name Hugh in several other plays. Eugene O'Neill, a broodingly atavistic Irish-American, was fascinated with and a captive of his own past. He preferred to think he could claim the heroic O'Neills of Tyrone as his heritage.

Considerable violence characterized the resistances in this and later periods, even though the punishment was often execution. But the long-range aim of holding Ireland subordinate to the English crown was attempted by various laws enacted during these years. Some of the laws, in addition to forbidding use of the Irish language, Irish dress, and Irish hair styles, also set forth limitations on Irish self-government. Just as Irish self-sufficiency in government threatened English supremacy, so, too, did Irish economic self-sufficiency; a poor Ireland was a safe Ireland. From the time of Henry VIII through the Penal Laws enacted in 1695, we can trace a deliberate English parliamentary effort to keep Ireland poor.

This discriminatory legislation forced the Irish to stay close to the land for subsistence. Whenever Ireland showed signs of developing any serious commercial enterprise, the English managed effectively, often with tariffs, to thwart that development. The Irish wool trade offers the clearest example. Ireland has much the same geography and climate as Scotland, and Scotland for centures has had a flourishing wool trade—Scottish wools, Scottish sweaters have long been sought after. But when Ireland began to develop a wool trade, the English inflicted high tariffs on the importation of Irish wool into England; the Irish wool trade was demolished. The Irish then shifted to linen, a trade never important enough to pose an economic threat to the English, so the trade in Irish linen survived. English policy of that sort kept Ireland an impoverished agrarian economy, with people living close to the soil, the kind of life that generates and sustains a vital and active folk imagination. This folk imagination continued in its individual Irish way as the rest of Europe developed economically and industrially.

During the time of Tudor expansion into Ireland, the Irish created many ballads. Many were lamentations about the time or expressed a romantic hope that help would come to Ireland to stem the difficulties. The Irish particularly hoped that help would come from Spain. One poem of the time that still survives in Irish memory is "Dark Rosaleen." Rosaleen personifies Ireland in the same way Uncle Sam stands for the United States or John Bull for England. Some verses from this poem, which originates in the 1500s, were translated from Gaelic into English by James Clarence Mangan, an Irish poet of the nineteenth century, another time of stirring for Irish independence, when a search for Irish roots was beginning anew. These stanzas come from Mangan's translation:

O, my Dark Rosaleen,
   Do not sigh, do not weep!
The priests are on the ocean green,
   They march along the Deep.
There's wine . . . from the royal Pope,
   Upon the ocean green;
And Spanish ale shall give you hope,
   My Dark Rosaleen!
   My own Rosaleen!
. . . .
Woe and pain, pain and woe,
   Are my lot, night and noon,
To see your bright face clouded so,
   Like to the mournful moon.
But yet . . . will I rear your throne
   Again in golden sheen;
'Tis you shall reign, shall reign alone,
   My Dark Rosaleen!
   My own Rosaleen!
'Tis you shall have the golden throne,
'Tis you shall reign, and reign alone,
   My Dark Rosaleen!
. . . .
I could scale the blue air,
   I could plough the high hills,
Oh, I could kneel all night in prayer,
   To heal your many ills!
And one . . . beamy smile from you
   Would float like light between

My toils and me, my own, my true,
  My Dark Rosaleen!
  My fond Rosaleen!
. . . .
O! the Erne shall run red
  With redundance of blood,
The earth shall rock beneath our tread,
  And flames wrap hill and wood,
  And gun-peal, and slogan cry,
  Wake many a glen serene.
Ere you shall fade, ere you shall die,
  My Dark Rosaleen!
  My own Rosaleen!
The Judgment Hour must first be nigh,
Ere you can fade, ere you can die,
  My Dark Rosaleen!

The lines combine bitter lamentation and strong national spirit. Not until Judgment Day will Dark Rosaleen be obliterated, and until that time the Irish will fight in many a glen serene.

Time and time again the English would come, confiscate Irish land, and push the Irish off to some other part of Ireland. After the "flight of the earls" in Ulster—the self-exile of almost a hundred defeated and disgruntled Irish rulers—King James I, Scottish-born successor to Henry VIII's daughter Queen Elizabeth I, confiscated in 1609 most of what is now Northern Ireland to establish what he clearly intended as a Protestant plantation. He took over virtually all of Ulster, expelling the Catholic population there and settling in Anglo-Scot Protestants. Already in 1609 we see the early roots of Ulster's present problems, and an early defining of the borders between Northern Ireland and the Irish Republic.

Soon after that, in 1642, the English deposed the then ruling king, Charles I, and from that time to 1660 the ruling force in England was the so-called rump Parliament, led by the controversial Oliver Cromwell. After Charles I was tried and beheaded in 1649, Cromwell turned his attention to Ireland. In an efficiently ferocious campaign famed for its flagrant cruelty, Cromwell's army captured vast stretches of land. Cromwell is said to have announced that the Irish could "go to hell or to Connaught"; to him they were both the same. Connaught, in the west of Ireland, often gets inclement weather and was for centuries one of the most impoverished areas of Ireland, a region where life was the hardest. Perhaps these migrations to Connaught created the present-day popular notion that the "real" Ireland is the west of Ireland, that the "real" Irish live there. Tourists still feel that to experience true Irish life they must find the "real" Irish peasantry who still live in small cottages and eke out their existence from an inhospitable land. In twentieth-century short stories Irish writers themselves frequently assert the West of Ireland to be the authentic Ireland, the place where an Irishman will find his roots. The short story writer and novelist Liam O'Flaherty often restored himself emotionally and psychologically by returning to the simplicity of the West.

Cromwell also brought into history Drogheda, a small city to the north of Dublin, by conducting a brutal massacre of its people in revenge for their resistance to England a few years earlier. A similar event occurred in the town of Wexford as well. These towns still remember those horrific times. A few years ago I happened to see a Hollywood film about Cromwell, extravagant in its praise of him, in a Dublin movie theater. I could feel the tension build and then burst into ridicule as the audience loudly rejected the elaborate protrayal of Cromwell as a representative of justice and democracy.

The next relevant date for us is 1690, the Battle of the Boyne. When the English deposed King James II in 1668, he fled to France, sympathetic Catholic France, to compose himself and to gather assistance to try to regain his throne. The English had selected William of Orange as their monarch. James decided to gather his forces in Ireland for an attack on England. Again notice the strategic importance of Ireland's position. William decided wisely enough not to confront James in England but to fight him in Ireland. After bringing his forces into friendly Ulster, William moved south seeking the enemy. In 1689 James had landed in the attractive small southern town of Kinsale, where he gathered his forces and started to move north. The opposing forces met in the middle of Ireland at the Boyne River, and there, in 1690, William of Orange defeated James. The date is significant in English history because the English Protestant monarchy, unsettled from the time of the Reformation, was finally secure. For Ireland the Battle of the Boyne produced yet another series of laws to punish Ireland. Land confiscations reduced to one-fifteenth the acreage in Ireland still owned by Irishmen. English overlords controlled the rest. The Penal Laws, enacted in 1695, assured English dominance and Protestant control of Ireland.

Some of the details of the Penal Laws illustrate their methods:

no Catholic could be in the Parliament, in the army, in the civil service, in the legal profession, in municipal corporations. Catholic children could not be educated abroad and the Protestant Church dominated education in Ireland. Catholics couldn't buy land from Protestants, and any Catholic who owned land had to, on his death, divide his land among his sons. However, if the eldest of the children decided to become a Protestant, all of the land immediately descended to that one child. Also, if a Protestant woman married a Catholic man, any land that she might own immediately went to her Protestant kin. Her ownership terminated with the marriage. Obviously such measures kept and increased the land under Protestant control.

At this time, as a consequence, great numbers of people began to leave Ireland. People of spunk, intelligence, or even genius, frequently decided that they must make their futures in lands other than in Ireland. Over these and other years those who left Ireland and went on to fame elsewhere included William Congreve, Oliver Goldsmith, Edmund Burke, and Richard Brinsley Sheridan. Ireland had lost some of its best people, and the leadership in Ireland passed to the clergy.

Education for Irish Catholics at home was available only in the "hedge-schools," which developed outside of the law, their name indicating the place of instruction, where the English overlords couldn't see the students and the teachers. While the subject matter was mainly classics and mathematics, often it was also the Irish language. Sometimes the teachers were Irish poets, who also passed on Irish lore and thus transmitted both an oral and written Irish heritage.

The oral tradition particularly informs the novel *Castle Rackrent* by Maria Edgeworth and to some extent, Swift's essay "A Modest Proposal." Historical events and the Penal Laws had turned Ireland into a two-class society. In the rest of Europe, certainly in England, a middle class—a commercial and trade class—had developed in size and strength. But in Ireland there were an uneducated peasant class of Irishmen and an upper class of landowners who were essentially English Protestants; only a small Catholic merchant class was sandwiched in between. An increasing peasant population intensified the dependence upon the land for its sustenance. Throughout the 1700s, Ireland's population increased rapidly. Indeed it doubled from an estimated two million people in 1700 to four million one hundred years later.

The increasing population, forced to split what land they had equally among the surviving sons, meant that more and more people had to survive on smaller and smaller parcels of land. The absentee landlords in England cared little about the land and tended to use it inefficiently. Poverty and starvation increased. It was now that the Irish turned to the potato to survive, since a plot of ground planted in potatoes yielded more sustenance than any other crop they knew. To feed the Irish population from grain crops at this time would have required an Ireland four times bigger than it was. This shift to, this near total dependence on, the potato would cause major difficulty in the nineteenth century.

From time to time throughout the 1700s, an individual potato crop would fail, affected by one plant disease or another. When this happened there was immediate hunger and frequent death from starvation. History tends to overlook these mini-famines because of the massive misery and starvation in Ireland between 1845 and 1848, when *every* potato crop failed for three years. The statistics of that time are so devastating, the wretchedness of conditions so astonishing, that we forget that in 1727 a crop failure caused 40,000 people to die of starvation. It was eighteenth-century conditions which provided the background for *Castle Rackrent* and for "Modest Proposal." The poor in Ireland were probably the most wretched in all of Europe — peasants huddled in one-room mud huts, the cows and pigs living with them of necessity, pools of rain water at the door, disease and epidemics widespread.

Superimposed on this misery was the grand life of the big house. Landlords, encouraged by a cheap labor supply, built sizable, often beautiful houses around the country. Many of them have since deteriorated or fallen into decay, but at the time they were very lavish. Such a big house provides the setting of *Castle Rackrent*.

But first let's look at Swift's short essay, "A Modest Proposal," published in 1729. Swift, an Anglican clergyman in Dublin who was angry and distressed by conditions in Ireland, clearly saw what was responsible for those conditions. His essay is a scorchingly angry response to what he saw around him daily. Part of the essay's literary brilliance and effectiveness comes from the fact that instead of directly denouncing the English policies Swift felt were responsible, he assumes "the persona" of an Englishman. He pretends that a rational, reasonable Englishman is making the modest proposal, a proposal typical of an Englishman's response to the wretched conditions in Ireland. The solution proposed reveals the kind of thinking that itself helps cause those conditions.

The persona employs what can be called English logic; he is materialistic and thinks, in a sense, reasonably. You will recall that I suggested earlier that Ireland was not touched by many of the economic and historical currents of Europe, and that the Irish retained a primitive imagination and a value system largely untouched by Western materialism. I also suggested that some of the practical logic and reason that crowded out imagination elsewhere had not affected the Irish quite so strongly. The persona of "A Modest Proposal" is very logical, but his logic is also very inhuman; and amazingly it doesn't ever occur to him that he is inhuman. He looks upon the Irish people as a commodity. He uses the language of trade in his proposal. He discusses the Irish as he might discuss a herd of cattle, using cattle terminology. He approaches the difficulties of Ireland with the logic of a businessman, and nothing more than the logic of a businessman.

He proposes, very calmly, to slaughter all Irish babies, fat babies he hopes, at one year of age, and to use them as food, perhaps for the Irish or for English ladies and gentlemen: "It is true, a child just dropped from its dam may be supported by her milk for a solar year, with little other nourishment; at most not above the value of 2s., which the mother may certainly get, or the value in scraps, by her lawful occupation of begging; and it is exactly at one year old that I propose to provide for them in such a manner as instead of being a charge upon their parents or the parish, or wanting food and rainment for the rest of their lives, they shall on the contrary contribute to the feeding, and partly to the clothing, of many thousands." The proposal has convincing logic about it, he says, because there's tremendous overpopulation in Ireland; slaughtering a lot of one-year-olds would save out a smaller number for breeding. Notice the cattle terminology. Secondly, the slaughter would provide food; it would reduce starvation in Ireland. How logical it all is! It never occurs to the proposer, though, that there is something wrong with slaughtering babies. Time and again Swift's persona calmly lists his reasons, using the terms of trade and business. Swift means, of course, exactly the opposite of what his persona says. By having the persona say what he says, Swift is exposing the point of view of the English, which he detests.

The essay illustrates the skill with which the Irish use language.

They carefully say one thing, intending, or meaning, something else. Irony, so expertly controlled by Swift, appears frequently in Irish literature. We see it in Maria Edgeworth's novel *Castle Rackrent*, which we will discuss next, and we find it all the way down to contemporary Irish writers like Samuel Beckett, whose depressing nihilism comes out in an opposite, comic mode. Swift employs irony not with fanciful lightness, but in white-hot anger. His satire is intense: his persona presents with calm self-assurance what is essentially inhuman logic. Swift is suggesting that the English are really devouring Ireland anyway and that this is one further illustration; Swift is noting that Irish children are better off being slaughtered than living in the miserable state of Ireland at the time. But most tellingly, Swift never allows the persona the slightest recognition of how inhuman and perverted are his suggestion and the values implicit in it.

In a lesser way Swift may also have been attacking the landlords of the time, whom he felt were not doing all they should. Swift very likely felt that landlords should be beneficient, helpful, good, and generous. And they were not. They were exactly the opposite, and that is part of Swift's complaint. Another enemy inherent in Swift's "A Modest Proposal" is the middle-class materialism that treats a problem in terms of trade instead of humanity.

One can trace through Irish literature right up to the present a distrust of the materialism of middle-class society. This distrust causes considerable tension in contemporary Irish culture because Ireland is now developing economically and has an increasing number of Irish middle class. Some recent Irish literature suggests that as people prosper, their hearts become hardened.

Another work reflecting the historical background that I've painted is Maria Edgeworth's novel *Castle Rackrent*. Maria Edgeworth was an English woman who came to live in Ireland, spending the last fifty-six of her eighty years there. *Castle Rackrent* was published in 1800, at the end of the eighteenth century, and may be looked upon in literary history as the first regional novel in English — a novel highlighting the characteristics of a certain area, in this instance Ireland, by focusing attention on the speech, customs, habits, and attitudes of a particular locale. Maria Edgeworth influenced the Scottish novelist Sir Walter Scott, who, impressed with what Maria Edgeworth did for Ireland, decided to do likewise for Scotland. *Castle Rackrent* may also be the first so-called saga novel in English literature, for in it the author takes a family and follows it through several generations.

Maria Edgeworth employs a technique in *Castle Rackrent* similar to Swift's: she adopts a persona, or a created character, to tell the story of the novel. The novel is really a string of anecdotes told by an Irish peasant, a man named Thady. Thady works for a series of English landlords in Castle Rackrent, the big house. Because Thady works for the family he has a skillfully developed ability to praise that family throughout the novel, to say "Oh, let me tell you how marvelous these people are." As he does so, though, he really means the reverse of what he is saying. This technique always reminds me of my old aunt, a meticulous housekeeper, who would say of a neighbor, "Isn't she wonderful. She's so carefree. Not a thing bothers her." What she meant was that the neighbor's children were running loose, that the house was a mess, and that there were dirty dishes in the sink. But she never said that. She said only something positive, but if one listened carefully to what was said positively, the full impact was the reverse.

Thady does the same in *Castle Rackrent*. He's been in the big house family's service for four generations, and on the surface his anecdotes seem to say how wonderful the family is, but the ultimate revelation is how absolutely mean-spirited and profligate they are. Thady, an Irish peasant, is uneducated, but he is very shrewd and knowledgeable in the ways of Irish life. He has what some call soft blarney. The reader recognizes that he's gotten along well by saying complimentary positive things. The peasant-landlord relationship makes it necessary for him to take this stance. It's rather like a black person in today's society "Uncle Toming it" ironically. Thady pretends to do and say all the right things, but something else is going on inside Thady all the time.

The novel opens with Thady speaking:

> Having, out of friendship for the family, upon whose estate,
> praise be Heaven! I and mine have lived rent free time out of
> mind, voluntarily undertaken to publish the MEMOIRS OF THE
> RACKRENT FAMILY, I think it my duty to say a few words,
> in the first place, concerning myself. My real name is Thady Quirk,
> though in the family I have always been known by no other than
> "Honest Thady."

3. Castletown House in County Kildare, a "big house," now maintained by the Irish Georgian Society. (Irish Tourist Board)

4. The ballroom in Castletown House. (Irish Tourist Board)

Notice immediately that Thady calls himself, Honest Thady. But, of course, he's not directly honest. He's playing a language game, saying one thing and meaning something else. For instance, here are some remarks he makes about one of the ladies of the house. Her maiden name, appropriately enough, was "Skinflint," and one of the Rackrents married her, thinking, foolishly, to get her money. Of this new mistress Thady says — notice how positively — the following:

> I must say for her, she made him the best of wives, being a very notable, stirring woman, and looking close to everything. But I always suspected she had Scotch blood in her veins; anything else I could have looked over in her, from a regard to the family. She was a strict observer, for self and servants, of Lent, and all fast-days, but not holidays. One of the maids having fainted three times the last day of Lent, to keep soul and body together, we put a morsel of roast beef into her mouth, which came from Sir Murtagh's dinner, who never fasted, not he; but somehow or other it unfortunately reached my lady's ears, and the priest of the parish had a complaint made of it the next day, and the poor girl was forced, as soon as she could walk, to do penance for it, before she could get any peace or absolution, in the house or out of it. However, my lady was very charitable in her own way. She had a charity school for poor children, where they were taught to read and write gratis, and where they were kept well to spinning gratis for my lady in return; for she had always heaps of duty yarn from the tenants, and got all her household linen out of the estate from first to last; for after the spinning, the weavers on the estate took it in hand for nothing, because of the looms my lady's interest could get from the Linen Board to distribute gratis. Then there was a bleachyard near us, and the tenant dare refuse my lady nothing, for fear of a lawsuit Sir Murtagh kept hanging over him about the water course. With these ways of managing, 'tis surprising how cheap my lady got things done, and how proud she was of it. Her table the same way, kept for next to nothing; duty fowls, and duty turkeys, and duty geese, came as fast as we could eat 'em, for my lady kept a sharp look-out, and knew to a tub of butter everything the tenants had, all round. They knew her way, and what with fear of driving for rent and Sir Murtagh's law suits, they were kept in such good order, they never thought of coming near Castle Rackrent without a present of something or other — nothing too much or too little for my lady — eggs, honey, butter, meal, fish, game, grouse, and herrings, fresh

or salt, all went for something. As for their young pigs, we had them, and the best bacon and hams they could make up, with all young chickens in the spring.

Notice the positive analysis Thady is presenting. That the lady of the house is so skillful and so careful and so close, she's really marvelous at it. What we learn, as he drops in little details, is that she's working the tenants at the looms pretending to teach them how to weave, but what she's really getting is all her linen free. That she keeps a sharp eye out so that she gets all the best bacon, geese, fowl, and butter from the whole area. How clever to be that able is Thady's point of view. But as we respond more thoughtfully to the reading, we notice that Thady is actually revealing the inexcusable Rackrenting operation of the lords of the big house and their treatment of the peasants. The novel sees clearly the realities of that era's two-class society.

A secondary theme of the novel concerns Thady's son Jason, who in the course of the novel develops into a land agent, one of the most typically hated characters in eighteenth- and nineteenth-century Irish fiction. A land agent represented the English landlord; he collected the rent from the Irish peasant, or, if the peasant didn't have the rent, actually evicted them from the house. In the course of the novel Jason cleverly manages to take over all of the Rackrent land, because the Rackrents themselves are so improvident. We learn throughout the novel that the Rackrent house is steeped in whiskey, drunkenness, decay, rot, pride, and improvidence, and Jason takes advantage of these faults to acquire a good deal of the Rackrent land. Thady, who may be responsible in a sense for helping his son take over the Rackrent property, says near the end of the novel — in an amusingly shrewd comment — that while he is embarrassed by the fact that his son has become a land agent, he's also rather satisfied that his son has now prospered: "I thought to make him a priest, but he did better for himself."

It remains a question when you finish the novel just how Maria Edgeworth actually felt about the Irish. She was certainly knowledgeable, and *Castle Rackrent* is one of the most revealing works of the eighteenth century.

CHAPTER THREE

Rebellions, Famine, Emigration

W E HAVE SEEN that by the eighteenth century Ireland's population was expanding tremendously, that English landlords owned well over 90 percent of the land, and that Ireland now had a two-class society: a class of peasants and a landlord class, called the Ascendancy. The first group was primarily Irish; the second group was essentially English. We also observed that the Irish farmers had come to rely upon a single crop, the potato, for their sustenance.

It's not surprising that the close of the eighteenth century should witness rising discontent among the people, and that there would be recurrent stirrings of resistance and rebellion—the same kind of resistance that occurred in the twelfth century when Henry II was granted Ireland as English territory, the same kind of resistance aimed against Henry VIII and Elizabeth I, the same kind of resistance that was sought to prevent James I's Ulster plantation, the same kind of resistance so savagely put down by Cromwell in the middle of the seventeenth century.

Conditions of life at the end of the eighteenth century generated in Ireland a major attempt at rebellion—the rebellion of '98. External factors also encouraged the attempt, for both the United States and France had successfully conducted revolutions and independence was in the air.

The rebellion which began in America in 1775 had particular relevance for Ireland. When England had to withdraw a considerable number of its troops from Ireland to send them to the colonial war, Ireland realized that the Irish should watch out for themselves. As early as 1778 the Irish began a volunteer army, one *not* under government control. It was really a land militia composed essentially of volunteers raised by landlords and by Protestant merchants who were agitated about English-originated trade restrictions in Ireland. A volunteer army outside of governmental control could still be said to flourish in present-day Irish tradition.

The American Revolution also brings into focus another Irish strategy: just as soon as England has difficulty somewhere else, the Irish should stage a rebellion. A new slogan was born — "England's trouble is Ireland's advantage." With England engaged in its American colonies, the time was ripe for Ireland to muster a rebellion. The group mostly responsible, the United Irishmen, was formed in 1791, in part through the efforts of a famous Irish hero, Wolfe Tone. Wolfe Tone was essentially an eighteenth-century rationalist, very much like the men who helped form the United States. A lawyer and a strong believer in democracy, Tone won support from the Irish and decided that it was the time for them to strike. The group hoped for French aid — French money, French arms — to support their cause, but only three days before the rebellion began, Napoleon determined on Egypt instead and sailed for Alexandria.

The Irish were left rather high and dry. The lack of French aid desperately undermined their effort, but the other factor contributing to the failure of the rebellion was the active spy network organized by the ruling authorities in Dublin Castle. Their information enabled the government to arrest the leaders on the eve of the revolt, which left the peasantry to fight leaderless. One of those arrested, the famous and dashing romantic figure Lord Edward Fitzgerald, remains a romantic hero in Irish lore to this day. Lord Edward Fitzgerald was a descendant of the Fitzgerald family which had resisted the English incursions in the fifteenth century. (Lord Edward Fitzgerald's handsome eighteenth-century townhouse on Dawson Street in Dublin now serves as the Irish Parliament building.) While the rebellion itself failed, many of its issues are still current in present-day Irish problems. A very strong national feeling, a feeling for national independence and unity, a feeling for democracy, as well as a good deal of social discontent inspired the Rebellion of '98. The peasantry rose up primarily because of the wretched and unfair conditions of their lives. Most of these elements recur in discussions of the problems in present-day Ulster.

Bernadette Devlin's book about her upbringing, *The Price of My Soul*, speaks of how the same strong and agitated social discontent propelled her into her political activity.

The Rebellion of '98 was essentially a handful of unfortunate military skirmishes in various parts of Ireland, primarily in County Wexford and in the west of Ireland. When the rebellion failed, most who took part were hanged.

From the '98 rebellion came a handful of ballads, most of them written about the deeds of the individual heroes, the deaths of the leaders, or the heroisms of particular battles.

One noteworthy ballad, "The Men of the West," tells of how a small French fleet sailed into Killala Bay to join the United Irishmen. (Ultimately they were forced to surrender). The ballad is a rousing one about the men waiting with their sticks for the exciting fight. A part of the song reflects the hopes of the peasantry:

> The hilltops of glory were glowing,
> 'Twas the eve of a bright harvest day.
> When the ships we'd been wearily waiting
> Sailed into Killala's broad bay,
> And over the hill went the slogan
> Awakening every breast.
> The Fire that has never been quenched, boys,
> Among the true hearts of the West.

The song cites towns in the west of Ireland—Ballina and Castlebar—and has an echoing refrain in praise of the men who fought there.

> When Ireland was broken and bleeding
> Hurrah for the men of the west.

Another song from the era is entitled "The Croppy Boy." Unlike the long-haired rebellious American youths in the 1960s, the Irish rebel tended to have his hair cut or cropped, hence the croppy boy. Fashionable hair styles of the men in power included long locks, so the boys with the short cuts rather than the boys with the pony tails were the rebels. In this song a croppy boy is going to be hanged for his rebellious activities. He has been caught because a cousin informed on him, and on the gallows he's renounced by his father. The song opens with an expression of the boy's hope for his country's freedom:

> It was very early in the spring,
> The birds did whistle and sweetly sing,
> Changing their notes from tree to tree,
> And the song they sang was Old Ireland free.

But the croppy boy is betrayed and taken prisoner and walked to the gallows, sadly passing his brother and sister. As he walks, he laments,

> As I was walking up Wexford Hill,
> Who could blame me to cry my fill?
> I looked behind and I looked before,
> But my tender mother I shall see no more.

> As I was mounted on the platform high,
> My aged father was standing by;
> My aged father did me deny,
> And the name he gave me was the Croppy Boy.

The song closes in mourning,

> It was in Dungannon this young man died,
> And in Dungannon his body lies;
> And you good Christians that do pass by
> Just drop a tear for the Croppy Boy.

Another Wexford song, "Boulavogue," named after the small town, focuses on the execution of Father Murphy, a rebel who fought at a place called Vinegar Hill. The rebel hands at the battle "set the heather blazing" for Ireland's freedom, but were defeated. Father Murphy was hanged and his "body burned on the rack." This song ends with a call for freedom:

> The cause that called you
> May call tomorrow
> In another fight
> For the green again.

"The Wind That Shakes the Barley," another touching lament from the 1798 rebellion, combines a love song with a rebel song. In it a rebel sings of how hard it is "to bear the shame of foreign chains around us." He determines to seek out the mountain glen "in the morning early and join the bold united men, while the soft wind shakes the barley." But tragedy hits as he says farewell to his love.

> While sad I kissed away her tears
> My fond arms round her clinging
> A foe man's shot burst on her ears
> From out the wild wood ringing.
> A bullet pierced my true love's side
> In life's young spring so early,
> And on my breast in blood she died,
> While soft winds shook the barley.

The song closes with the grieving rebel at the grave of his dead love.

In addition to these musical, and somewhat literary results, the revolt produced political effects as well. The English dissolved Irish Parliament and determined to govern Ireland directly from London. They formed—and this is the beginning of the term—the United Kingdom of Great Britain and Ireland. The Anglican Church was renamed the United Church of England and Ireland, and an overall effort sought to strengthen union of Ireland with England, even, perhaps, to overcome Irishness altogether. When we read carefully the preface to Maria Edgeworth's *Castle Rackrent*, written in 1800, we see that one reason she wrote this regional novel was because she expected Irishness soon to disappear, and she wanted to record it in her novel. The pertinent sentences read as follows:

> When Ireland loses her identity by an union with Great Britain,
> she will look back, with a smile of good-humored complacency,
> on the Sir Kits and Sir Condys of her former existence.

Of course Ireland did not lose its sense of identity as a result of the United Kingdom, nor have the Irish been able to look back with a smile on the English landlords of the eighteenth century.

In the nineteenth century the strides toward Irish nationhood occurred primarily through political maneuvering rather than through military rebellion. Two leaders of great political skill came forth in Ireland in this period — Daniel O'Connell in the first half of the century, Charles Stewart Parnell, in the latter half.

Daniel O'Connell is, of course, one of the great Irish political heroes. He strove, especially with his electric oratorical skill and shrewd political maneuvering, to unite the Irish and to win political concessions from England. England responded somewhat more sympathetically at this time because the country was itself becoming more democratic through the series of reform bills enacted in this period. Daniel O'Connell's pressure and the spirit of the times caused London to lift most important restrictions on the Irish. Roman Catholics were allowed to sit in Parliament beginning in 1829. Then, with the enfranchisement of most Roman Catholics, O'Connell was also able to pressure the British into granting Ireland an elementary education system. In the eighteenth century the education system was in the hands of the Church of England. With the possibilities of a broader education system Ireland could now begin to have a literate populace. With this great achievement came one great loss, however. The education Daniel O'Connell fought so hard to win was conducted in the English language. Since the invasions of Henry II in the twelfth century the Gaelic language had managed to hang on as the native tongue of Irishmen. But during the 1800's fewer and fewer people spoke Gaelic as English, for the first time, took over. It's an irony that Daniel O'Connell helped bring about the loss of the Gaelic tongue. The potato famine in mid-century also devasted Irish-speaking areas.

In the first half of the nineteenth century one of the main Irish literary figures is Thomas Moore. Thomas Moore was one of those who found it more beneficial for his own development to leave Ireland and spend most of his life in England. Dublin-born, he became popular as a poet and as a singer of national airs after his move to England. In the early part of the nineteenth century there was a popular interest throughout Europe in songs or airs reflecting national identifications. You find, for instance, Byron's *Hebrew Melodies* developing national airs of the Middle East. Walter Scott was doing the same thing with Scottish material. Thomas Moore composed a number of Irish airs that he called the *Irish Melodies*, and they are among the most popular poems and songs of the early nineteenth century. Thomas Moore himself was the toast of a large segment of English society. One must remember that poetry was a very popular literary form in the nineteenth century. Unlike most people today a sizable number of people in nineteenth-century England read poetry regularly.

The *Irish Melodies* remain known, and I think it's correct to say, remain loved by the Irish to this day. Literary critics and scholars have somewhat neglected and snubbed these songs because of their supposedly melancholy sentimentality, but all of us know some of the Irish melodies even if we don't realize it. The song, "Last Rose of Summer," for instance, is one; so too is "Believe Me If All Those Endearing Young Charms."

Thomas Moore was very skilled in poetic technique. The lyrics and the music have a graceful and beautiful tone, a soft and melancholy mood. Thomas Moore precedes the English poet Alfred Tennyson, who wrote in the latter part of the century, but some think Moore to be the equal, perhaps even the superior of Tennyson in some instances, especially in his lyric ability to create a slow and graceful melancholic mood.

Thomas Moore did contribute poetry that had the spirit of Irish nationalism in it as well. These poems, that catch the stirrings, the rekindling of the desire for independence in the early part of the nineteenth century, are worth noting. One well-known example is "The Minstrel Boy." The first stanza tells that the Minstrel Boy has gone to war and joined the ranks of the dead, with "his wild harp slung behind him." The second stanza denounces the slavery that has silenced the harp:

> The minstrel fell!—but the foeman's chain
>   Could not bring his proud soul under;
> The harp he lov'd ne'er spoke again,
>   For he tore its chords asunder;
> And said, "No chains shall sully thee,
>   "Thou soul of love and bravery!
> "Thy songs were made for the pure and free,
>   "They shall never sound in slavery!"

The harp as an Irish national symbol is clear enough, and Moore is far from subtle about the source of the slavery, though he never states it. The harp recurs in other Moore songs.

More explicitly in the mood of Thomas Moore is the lyric "The

5. The monument to Daniel O'Connell in O'Connell Street, Dublin. On close
inspection at the monument, bullet holes from gunfire in the 1916 rising can be seen.

6. The poet Thomas Moore. (Irish Tourist Board)

Harp That Once Through Tara's Halls." In this poem Moore goes back to the ancient Irish kingdom with its headquarters at Tara. The harp in this song may recall the harp of the old Irish leader Brian Boru, though he is never mentioned, but in any case the harp is again a national symbol. Moore laments that the harp that once sang through Tara's Halls no longer plays.

> The harp that once through Tara's halls
>   The soul of music shed,
> Now hangs as mute on Tara's walls,
>   As if that soul were fled. —
> So sleeps the pride of former days,
>   So glory's thrill is o'er,
> And hearts, that once beat high for praise,
>   Now feel that pulse no more!
> No more to chiefs and ladies bright
>   The harp of Tara swells;
> The chord, alone, that breaks at night,
>   Its tale of ruin tells.
> Thus freedom now so seldom wakes,
>   The only throb she gives,
> Is when some heart indignant breaks,
>   To shew that still she lives.

Notice the melancholic tone typical of Moore, coupled with the lamentation for the apparent lack of freedom in Ireland. The only time that the Harp of Tara swells is when a heart breaks merely to show that freedom still lives in that breaking heart.

One would expect, given such beginnings, that a stronger move for Irish independence would appear by the mid-nineteenth century. Instead catastrophe struck. The famine from 1845 until 1848 overshadowed all stirrings for independence. It had not been unusual for individual potato crops to fail, or even for two. From 1727 to 1729 and in 1740 and 1741 there was extensive crop failure. In 1816 hunger struck large parts of Ireland because of crop failure. In these years thousands died from starvation and disease. But between 1845 and 1848 all potato crops failed. Crop after crop, year after year, fell to disease.

The extent of the potato famine and its effects on the culture and literature of Ireland are such that all we can do is outline basic elements to indicate what a massive disaster that it was. Those seeking a full and thoughtful study of this disaster should read *The Great Hunger* by the English historian Cecil Woodham-Smith. Historians estimate that at least a million people died of starvation or disease in those particular years. Enormous numbers of Irish, of course, emigrated; indeed it's the potato famine that initiates emigration as a major continuing factor of Irish life. Only in recent years has the birth rate in Ireland exceeded the emigration rate. From 1845 until a few years ago Ireland's population declined; more people were dying in or leaving Ireland than were born there.

Those who emigrated during the famine were often afflicted by disease; most were forced to leave their homes because they couldn't pay their landlords the profit from their crops, which was their rent. Throughout the years evictions, often of the weak and ill, were legion. At this time the English pursued a *laissez-faire* economic policy, which dictated that left alone, the economy would work out correctly. Leaving it alone meant to the English enforcing the system that they had, so if Irish tenants could not pay their rent, English soldiers would march up to evict them from their households. Time and time again English soldiers would appear, set fire to the thatched roofs, and knock in the sides of the cottages with battering rams. Often the English soldiers had to lift starving, diseased, and sometimes dying, people from the cottages and carry them out into the roadways. The roads of Ireland were littered with people dying from starvation and crowded with others trying to get to the coast or to go somewhere where they could get some kind of sustenance.

The English came to terms rather slowly with the fact that masses of Irish were starving. In 1847 they instituted a program of public works so that the Irish could earn some income. Also in 1847 they established soup kitchens to relieve the starvation. Folk stories, true or untrue, have been handed down about some of these kitchens. One story focuses on the soup kitchens set up by Protestant missionary societies; if the Irish Catholics wanted to have the soup, they had to sign a pledge that they would convert to Protestantism. The Irish called those who did Soupers.

Because British *laissez-faire* economics dictated that relief should not be the function of government, what the English did was utterly insufficient. And the English never did face the basic economic problems, including an absentee landlord class, which had contributed to the difficulty in the first place.

The famine changed the landscape of Ireland as significantly as it changed the landscape of the United States. Population in Ireland dropped from an estimated eight million in 1841 to an estimated six-and-a-half million ten years later. By 1871 only five-and-a-half milion people remained in Ireland, with emigration reducing that number every year.

Irish farmers turned away from the potato, from tillage farming in general, and began to develop a grazing agriculture. This tended to hasten emigration also because grazing requires less labor than crop tillage. It's at this time that Ireland begins providing England with beef and dairy products, which are among Ireland's main products to this day.

Of course the emigration changed the political and cultural landscape of the United States also. Great waves of immigrants came to Boston, to Philadelphia, to New York City, to Albany, to Buffalo, and to places farther west, including California, with its lure of gold. Many cities in the United States rather quickly tried to prevent the afflicted Irish from landing. The ships themselves were death ships. Disease was rampant, cholera and dysentery raged on board. The cities of the United States, especially Boston, could scarcely absorb the great numbers of people that were coming. Boston was a relatively small city without housing facilities for the swarms of impoverished people who landed there. All the problems that the Irish brought were ones that the Irish-Americans strove to solve through political pressure and political manipulations, action which eventually helped bring about changes in the focus of governmental concern. Many of the social welfare programs and the public parks, schools, and hospitals that developed in the United States came about primarily because the waves of immigration made them desparately needed.

It's almost impossible to find satisfactory contemporary literary reflections about the potato famine. We can only assume that contemporary writers were probably suppressing its horror. Interestingly enough twentieth century Irish writers are trying to face that task, are giving their attention to the potato famine in historical fiction. Walter Macken's novel *The Silent People* brings the reader to the brink of the potato famine and then stops, perhaps because Macken feels unable to express the full emotional reality of the disaster itself. Liam O'Flaherty's novel, *Famine*, which has not been easy to obtain, is perhaps the most effective.

Nineteenth-century literature contains a number of fictional scenes, primarily heart-rending encounters, dealing directly with evictions. Although scholars have tended to overlook nineteenth-century Irish literature, one of the strongest scenes dealing with evictions appears in *Valentine McClutchy,* a novel by William Carleton. Carleton's writings were popular among the Irish in the late nineteenth century, but they are now mostly out of print.

In chapter 8 we will examine a short story that I think is the best, the most touching story dealing with emigration and the pains of leaving one's homeland forever. The story, "Going Into Exile," is by Liam O'Flaherty and focuses on the feelings of a family as a young brother and sister leave their household to come to the United States. The family hold a little party the night before, what the Irish call an American wake, since it's apparent that the brother and sister will never see their family again. Nowadays the Irish who emigrate can be pretty certain that they're going to earn enough for an excursion airfare home to visit in a year or two. In the nineteenth and early twentieth century when somebody left home it was almost certain they would never see any of their family again. It's this mood and this emotion that Liam O'Flaherty captures in "Going Into Exile."

Brian Friel's recent play called "Philadelphia Here I Come," a Broadway hit some years ago, deals with the interior feelings of a young lad who is leaving Ireland for Philadelphia.

The emotional turmoil of emigration became engrained in the consciousness of generations of Irish-Americans.

CHAPTER FOUR

Parnell and Cathleen ni Houlihan

As WE MOVE into the later nineteenth and early twentieth century, a period rich in fascinating historical details which sees the birth of the Celtic Literary Renaissance and its efflorescence of great writers, the connections between history and literature grow even stronger than they have been in the material that we have dealt with thus far. It took, however, a few decades after the famine of 1845-48 for the Irish and for Ireland to recover energy and to assert once again its own national identity.

At first the various movements towards national identity were rather isolated and fragmented individual concerns, but later they unified into a single, nationalistic political force. In 1870 Isaac Butt founded one of the more significant of these individual groups, the Home Rule League. Precisely as its name suggests, the League sought to have Ireland govern itself again. This did not mean that Ireland should govern itself *independently*, but rather that it should have its own parliament, as it had until 1800, when the Irish Parliament was dissolved and the Parliament in London assumed direct control.

Another significant group was the Land League, begun in 1879 by Michael Davitt. The Land League sought to protect tenants from eviction and from the high rents of the landlords, whose power we noted in *Castle Rackrent*. While that novel described conditions in the eighteenth century, a similar state of affairs existed in the nineteenth century.

Initially these two groups functioned independently of one another, but the second major political figure of the nineteenth century brought them together. We saw how Daniel O'Connell dominated the first half of the nineteenth century; the second half of the century provided the stage for that other major political figure, Charles Stewart Parnell. Parnell, with shrewd political skill, molded the Home Rule League, the Land League, and several other groups into a single political force. In that alliance was born a new assertion of national strength, dominated and directed by Parnell.

Parnell's primary stated purpose, as he gathered these fragmented groups together, was to get home rule for Ireland — a system in which Ireland would govern itself under the Crown of England. But Parnell may have had eventual nationhood in mind for Ireland. In one speech, for instance, he claimed, "No man has the right to fix the boundary of the march of a nation."

Throughout the nineteenth century England frequently supported movements for national independence. The English supported, for instance, the movement for Italian independence in the early part of the nineteenth century. The English author Shelley participated in this effort. And Lord Byron lost his life in the struggle for Greek independence. Similarly the English supported movements for Polish independence and for Serbian independence. Nonetheless the English resisted giving any independence or home rule to Ireland. Although willing to give home rule to Canada, to Australia, and to other parts of the British Commonwealth, England opposed according similar rights to Ireland. When historians speculate as to why, they arrive at economic and strategic reasons. Ireland provided a necessary market for English goods; it had also become a necessary source of food for England. After the potato famine, when Ireland shifted to dairy farming, Ireland became England's larder. London preferred to keep its food under close scrutiny. Also, Ireland continued to have strategic value for England. Its proximity to England made it all too tempting a site from which to launch an attack on England. That had certainly been true in the Renaissance period and in late Stuart times when ousted King James II mustered his forces in Ireland, only to lose the fight at the Battle of the Boyne. The wars of the twentieth century again demonstrated the strategic importance of Ireland.

As the move for Home Rule progressed under Parnell, most people in Ireland supported him. The Ulsterites, however, resisted Home Rule very strongly, for their industry depended heavily on England, and because they feared that "home rule is Rome rule."

Parnell himself was an Anglo-Irish Protestant and so too was Isaac Butt, who had formed the Home Rule League, but while the people in southern Ireland generally supported the Protestant leaders seeking home rule, the people in the north did not. Protestantism in the North tended to be Presbyterian (many lowland Scot Presbyterians had emigrated there from nearby Scotland) whereas Protestantism in the rest of Ireland tended to be Church of England. But probably the strongest factor generating resistance in Ulster was that the North of Ireland had developed industrially more than the rest of Ireland. While it is evident that the English did not want Ireland to achieve any kind of national strength, or threat, through economic development, the North, through various political mechanisms and because of "safe" constituency, had managed to get more comfortable economic allowances from the Crown. Industry, for instance shipbuilding, had prospered in the North. The economy of the North, which differed considerably from that of the rest of Ireland, made union with England more advantageous than home rule. The economic realities in Ireland have always been intriguing, and they still very profoundly affect present-day difficulties.

It's paradoxical that the move for and achievement of national independence came at a time of growing economic interdependence between England and Ireland. Today the Common Market has brought the Irish Republic into an economic union with England. Simultaneously in the last several decades Ireland has asserted its national identity and has begun to develop industrially with the aid of foreign investments. What effect a developed economy in the Irish Republic will have on its political relations with the North remains to be seen. In any case in Parnell's time the move for home rule had its opponents.

Parnell was a compelling historical figure; his life has received outstanding treatment in a recent biography F.S.L. Lyons of Trinity College, Dublin. Parnell not only dominated the political scene, but he also exerted a great influence on the literature of the period and the spirit of the times from which that literature drew. His life story, his personality, his bearing, form the stuff not only of history but of poetry, drama, and fiction. He became a kind of mythological figure, if you wish. He was tall and apparently quite aloof, an aristocratic gentleman with an aristocratic bearing, the kind of person that apparently the Irish could look to with admiring pride. He was not the kind of man who could walk, as the Irish would say, with cabbages and kings. He wasn't very good about the cabbages, but his bearing seemed appropriate for a leader. Parnell's advocacy of home rule appeared to have won sympathetic response in Parliament, especially from Prime Minister Gladstone, who had come to favor home rule for Ireland. This fact, along with Parnell's political skill, suggested that Ireland would soon gain home rule. However, some rather interesting and intriguingly complicated events prevented that.

At Christmas time in 1889, to the great surprise of the Irish, one Captain William O'Shea filed for divorce from his wife Kitty and cited Parnell as the co-respondent. That aloof, cool, seemingly passionless Parnell had been having a long-term sexual relationship with Kitty O'Shea completely shocked and scandalized the Irish. To assess the extent of the shock, we must remember that we are dealing with an essentially puritanical people in the late Victorian age. They were absolutely outraged. It's an intriguing question why Captain O'Shea happened to file for divorce so ostentatiously at this time, for the affair had been going on for some time. Was someone, perhaps an Englishman, trying to wreck Parnell's political efforts or had Captain O'Shea simply decided he'd had enough? That's a kind of back-room history that we can't explore, but it is curious that Captain O'Shea brought his case on Christmas Eve 1889. The divorce came to court the following November, and two days later, on November 17th the divorce was granted.

On November 18th the National League, the political constituency Parnell had formed, pledged its continuing support to him and the following week, on November 25th, the leaders of the Irish Parliamentary Party met to consider whether they wished this somewhat "immoral" man to continue as their leader. That day they gave him an immediate vote of confidence. But the next day they reconsidered, questioning whether the scandal endangered his effectiveness as a leader. Debate continued until December 6th. When the ballots on that vote of confidence were counted, Parnell learned that his party had decided by a vote of 44 to 26 to terminate his chairmanship.

What appears to have wrought the change was this. After the original vote of confidence on November 25th Prime Minister Gladstone, forced by his own constituency of English liberals, told the Irish that if they continued to have such an immoral man as Parnell as leader, then he, Gladstone, could not continue to support

Home Rule. The Irish Parliamentary Party began meeting again the next day to reconsider their vote. Parnell himself tried very hard to hang on to his leadership. He felt very strongly that the English should not dictate to the Irish who their leader should be. During those ten days when debate raged, the sophisticated and the intellectuals of Dublin tended to support Parnell strongly. However on December 3rd the Catholic Church in Ireland denounced Parnell. With that Parnell had lost his necessary support; he could no longer lead effectively. That the Church withdrew its support from Parnell still engenders a certain amount of bitter feeling among many Irish, who feel that the Church helped to demolish the movement for Home Rule at that time.

The great Irish writer James Joyce wrote: "They did not throw him to the English wolves, they tore him to pieces themselves." It's an irony of history that the Irish, whatever the impetus from the English, themselves destroyed the strongest and most effective leader they had had in fifty years.

A politically broken man, Parnell was also a sick man. The following year, in 1891, he died, at the rather young age of 45. With his death, which appeared to have washed away his sins, Parnell became a tragic hero in Irish political history, and as such is revered by the Irish.

Since we are discussing Irish culture, as well as history and literature, we can take a little byway and talk about graveyards. The Irish love graveyards. Certainly it's only an Irish girl who understands that if an Irish boy takes her to a cemetery and says "Would you like to lie with my people," that he's actually proposing marriage. Parnell's grave is in the major cemetery of Dublin, Glasnevin Cemetery. While it has many marvelous graves, it's all very congested and close together, a forest of tombstones. But when you come to Parnell's grave, there is a bit of a clearing. The grave is just a mound of dirt in this circular clearing, with a very low iron chain fence around it and a great, huge rock from the Wicklow Mountains, where Parnell was born, placed on the mound. A small sign identifies Parnell as "The Chief."

One reason I mention Parnell's grave is to point out that while the Irish were scandalized and shocked by Parnell, once he died, he in a sense redeemed himself. The Irish reverted to their former admiration and high regard for him and for the national movement that he represented. So in a peculiar sort of way, Parnell's death

7. The monument to Charles Stewart Parnell in upper O'Connell Street, (Irish Tourist Board)

gave further impetus to his cause and in a sense he continued to accomplish his goals when he was dead as well as he might have had he lived. A whole mythology grew up about Parnell; he figures frequently in Irish literature, and an increased energy and idealism arises in Irish politics and literature largely because of Parnell.

Later, when we talk about Yeats, we will consider a poem he published in 1914 called, "To a Shade," which describes the shade, or spirit, of Parnell. In another poem, "The Fisherman," Yeats creates an image of a strong, tall, aloof fisherman, who is in control, passionless, and hard-bitten on the exterior but inside has a tremendous passion which is restrained only by the strength of his personality. Certainly this seems very much like the personality of Parnell, who appeared aloof and aristocratic and yet who was, underneath, a man of great passion. (At least so we must suppose.) But the Irish memory of Parnell becomes a vital element in the spirit of the times and informs much of the literature. Hence Parnell lives not merely as an historical figure but as a very significant literary one as well.

Thus far we've looked at some events in Irish history, and then given attention to the literature that grew from, or reflected them. At this point, however, that pattern reverses itself. Instead of literature reflecting history, literature begins to *cause* the history. Writers actually stimulate some of the tumultous events of the twentieth century. When we look at the Easter Rising in 1916, we will see that several of its leaders were poets and schoolteachers, not military men (which may explain why the Rebellion failed). A number of vital writers appeared at the end of the nineteenth century whose strong and lofty idealism fired the imagination of the Irish people to strive again for national independence. So, rather than look at historical events and then at literature, we'll now examine the literature and connect it to the events it inspires.

Among the writers at the turn of the century is a lesser writer, but a notable one, who illustrates the power of the pen in Ireland at this time. A philologist at University College, Dublin, Douglas Hyde became very concerned that spoken Gaelic was going out of usage in Ireland. In an attempt to save the Gaelic tongue and to make it Ireland's national language, Hyde became the first president of the Gaelic League, a group formed by Eoin Mac Neill to promote, or even just to salvage, the use of the spoken Gaelic. But eventually that Gaelic League came to foster the use of anything Gaelic, anything that distinguished the Irish from the English. It evolved into a force that said, "Let's not be like the English. Let's be Irish in every way we can possibly think of." Another group, the Gaelic Athletic League, formed to encourage Gaelic athletic activities rather than English athletic games. A spectator can still detect the differences not only between games as they are played in Ireland and England — a Gaelic football game is quite different from a Rugby match — but there's a distinction between the crowds at the games as well. One leader of the 1916 Rebellion, Patrick Pearse, claimed that the Gaelic League had strongly influenced his activities.

Douglas Hyde, in addition to starting the Gaelic League, also wrote an influential essay entitled "The Necessity For De-Anglicizing Ireland" in which he suggested that the Irish not ape the English in any way. And in his concern for the Gaelic tongue, Hyde collected a group of Gaelic poems called *The Love Songs of Connaught*, which he translated into English. The volume printed the Gaelic on one side of the page and the English on the other. There they were, side by side. This book helped convince the English that there really was a worthwhile Gaelic literature. The English tended to think that the Irish were living with chickens and pigs in awful little cottages, that they certainly were incapable of producing any rich or valuable literary heritage. But these poems, the English translations side by side with the Gaelic, gave impetus to the recognition that there really was a valuable Irish literature.

The turn of the nineteenth century also witnessed the beginnings of Irish theater. Until the 1890s, there really was no indigenous theater in Ireland. While Irish stories were highly dramatic, there were no plays. Those plays which were performed in Dublin in the eighteenth and nineteenth centuries were usually put on by travelling companies from England, most bringing popular, commercial English music hall productions. Hyde wanted to develop Gaelic theater, or at least Gaelic playwriting. To which end he wrote in Gaelic a one-act play, a somewhat slight folk story in which a bumpkin is outwitted by some shrewd folk, "The Twisting of the Rope." Yeats had suggested using this old Irish story as the scenario for the play. It is the first play that we know of in the Gaelic language. At about the same time William Butler Yeats, one of the world's great literary figures, decided that there should be some Irish theater. Among other things Yeats hoped an Irish theater would offer something more aesthetically challenging than the vulgarity or razzmatazz of English music hall. He first wrote a one-act play called "The Land of the Heart's Desire," which he produced in London in 1894.

At the turn of the century Yeats wrote another play, called "Cathleen ni Houlihan." A one-act play like "Land of The Heart's Desire," this work is a powerful drama of major significance which helped inspire the Rebellion of 1916. It was first performed in 1902 in Dublin, in a little auditorium, St. Theresa's Hall. Yeats claimed that the idea for the play came to him in a dream, perhaps inspired by Dublin's celebration of the centenary of the 1798 Rebellion. The banners in the streets and the parades may have suggested to Yeats some of the subject matter for "Cathleen ni Houlihan." The play takes place in 1798, in a small cottage near Killala Bay in Sligo.

The play essentially concerns a love triangle. That doesn't sound very Irish, but it's a particular kind of love triangle. On the eve of his marriage to a girl named Delia Cahill a young man named Michael Gillane is talking with his family in the cottage about the advantages of this marriage, particularly the financial advantage, since Delia Cahill is bringing with her a hundred pound dowry. Then a strange old woman, who seems to the family even a little daft, appears at the cottage. The woman, Cathleen ni Houlihan, clearly represents or personifies the spirit of Ireland. She talks somewhat oddly and mysteriously and symbolically, but the audience, especially an Irish audience, knows exactly what she's talking about and exactly what she represents. She's talking about fighting and dying for Ireland in the upcoming 1798 Rebellion as she speaks lines like this: "But when trouble is on me I must be talking to my friends." When one of the people in the cottage asks why she is wandering, the old woman answers, "Too many strangers in the house," referring, of course, to the English. One person comments, "Indeed you look as if you'd had your share of trouble." "I have had trouble indeed," she responds. "What was it put the trouble on you?" she is asked. The old woman answers, "My land that was taken from me." The question "Was it much land they took from you?" draws her answer, "My four beautiful green fields." The four beautiful green fields are of course the four ancient counties of Ireland — Leinster, Munster, Ulster, and Connaught.

After those lines she sings a little song — Irish plays often contain music — and she speaks of dead Irish patriots, Brian Boru and

Red Hugh O'Donnell, citing them as representative of people who "died of love for me." "Many a man has died for love of me," she exclaims. And then she exhorts, "If anyone would give me help he must give me himself, he must give me all."

Michael Gillane, the groom-to-be, is so moved by these statements and so transfixed by the spell that Cathleen ni Houlihan casts, that he decides to forgo marriage — to join with Cathleen ni Houlihan and to forsake Delia Cahill. Love for country and Cathleen ni Houlihan wins out over Delia and home. He vows to join Cathleen, and she says:

> It is a hard service they take that help me. Many that are red cheeked now will be pale-cheeked; many that have been free to walk the hills and the bogs and the rushes will be sent to walk hard streets in far countries; many a good plan will be broken; many that have gathered money will not stay to spend it; many a child will be born and there will be no father at its christening to give it a name. They that have red cheeks will have pale cheeks for my sake, and for all that, they will think they are well paid.

Michael is mesmorized by this nationalistic idealism, though his family pleads with him to stay, to marry Delia Cahill, to be comfortable on the farm in the cottage. But he and the old woman leave the cottage. As they're walking away, one member of the family asks, "Did you see the old woman going down the path?" And the answer comes back, "I did not, but I saw a young girl, and she had the walk of a queen." At the very end of the play Cathleen ni Houlihan is transformed, for the 1798 Rebellion which is going to take place the next day. The spirit of Ireland is reborn.

Although written in prose, the play has the strong emotional effectiveness of poetry. It's a stirring articulation of Irish nationalism, a dramatic call to arms. Many of the people who saw the play in 1902 and subsequent productions felt called upon to give themselves for Ireland in the way that Michael Gillane had given himself in the play. After the 1916 Rebellion, when the leaders had been executed and the other dead buried, Yeats felt some guilt or at least responsibility for the deaths that had occurred. His play, he knew, had driven his Irish audience to action. Indeed the Abbey Theatre chose to commemorate the deaths of the leaders immediately after their execution with a production of "Cathleen ni Houlihan."

CHAPTER FIVE

Strumpet City: Strike, Lockout, Distress

L ABOR UNREST also fueled the growing nationalism. Ireland's labor movement lagged a bit behind that in the rest of the world—that frequently happens in Ireland—and labor unrest surfaced in the United States and in England several decades before it did in Ireland. But discontent there comes as no surprise. In that essentially two-class society, the working conditions and poor pay engendered resentment and opposition within the poorer class. The unrest grew until in August 1913 the Irish Transport and General Workers Union led an important labor strike. Two wonderfully interesting leaders of the Irish labor movement, James Larkin, called "Big Jim," and James Connolly are called up to this day as an inspirational force in some of the job and civil rights difficulties in the North. The employers rallied very strongly around one leader, a man named William Martin Murphy.

William Martin Murphy, somewhat cruelly trying to strangle the labor movement at its birth, called, early in fall 1913, for a lockout of all workers sympathetic with labor unions; wages ceased and work slowed. The eight-month lockout led to a desperate period in Dublin, for workers were earning nothing. Living conditions had always been marginal at best, but in those weeks the hunger bordered on starvation. So dreadful did life become that the workers developed a plan to send their children to England until the strike was over because the children were not getting fed properly. The scheme was opposed, however, by the Church hierarchy in Dublin, who feared that Protestants would proselytize the children. The employers' lockout generally succeeded but it did serve to unify workers more completely than they had ever achieved on their own.

One event from this period lives on in the people's memory. On August 31, 1913, the workers called for a peaceful demonstration to show their unity and strength. When the demonstrators assembled on what was then called Sackville Street, now O'Connell Street, the major street in the center of Dublin, the police, including the Royal Irish Constabulary, marched on the crowd of men, women, and children and beat them savagely with relentless, indiscriminate fury. The event absolutely horrified the Irish, who called the day Bloody Sunday. The fact that *Irish* police turned on *Irish* workers and their families in the 1913 demonstration particularly agitated the population at large. And historians quite rightly feel that the Bloody Sunday and the Labor Movement helped galvanize the forces drawing the Irish together and moving them toward the Easter Rebellion of 1916.

The years of the labor movement from 1909 to the strike of 1913 in Dublin serve as the background for James Plunkett's historical novel entitled *Strumpet City*, published in 1969. An extremely readable book popular in Ireland and the United States, this novel presents a compelling and probably quite accurate picture of life in Dublin at the time. It comprehends within its scope the various class levels in Ireland at the time and skillfully weaves notable historical figures such as Jim Larkin into the background. We see in *Strumpet City* the emergence in Ireland of a three-class system. Where before Ireland had contained an upper class, the Ascendancy, and a lower class, the peasants, the twentieth century witnessed the formation of a new working, middle class. A change transmutes the social framework and class structure in Ireland.

The action of *Strumpet City* takes place from 1909 to 1914; the author focuses mainly on the living conditions at various levels of society in Dublin, on the growing labor movement, on the details of the lockout and the strike, and the aftermath of these events at the beginning of World War I.

The novel's historical background includes not only the Dublin transportation strike but various minor riots inspired by political fervor. One, for instance, came in response to a production of the Yeats' nationalistic play, "Cathleen ni Houlihan." Also interwoven into the plot are tales from that period's active and significant women's movement. Plunkett portrays some of the notable suffragette leaders, including Maud Gonne, who played Cathleen in

Yeats' "Cathleen ni Houlihan," and Countess Marciewicz, who also became active in the labor movement and who helped lead the 1916 Rebellion. Arrested for her activities in 1916, she was sentenced to death, but through an ironic twist of sexism was not executed as were the other, male leaders.

Other historical figures who figure in the background of *Strumpet City* are the admirable labor leader Jim Larkin, the villainous William Martin Murphy, who led the employers into declaring the lockout, and Edward Carson, an important Ulster Orangeman who shaped English-Irish political relations in the period from 1912 to 1914. The best book on this critical period in Irish and English politics was written by George Dangerfield. Called *The Strange Death of Liberal England*, Dangerfield's study focuses attention on the skill that Edward Carson used in forcing the Ulster cause on English politics. Although the Ulsterites were a small faction, they could swing votes in English politics, to either the Tories or the Whigs. Dangerfield also wrote *The Damnable Question*, which treats the Irish question more broadly. A most skilled and beautiful writer of history, Dangerfield's works cannot come too highly recommended.

While important historical personages crowd the background in *Strumpet City*, the novel concentrates on the life and the living conditions of fictional characters. Plunkett presents an array of characters from various levels and classes of Dublin life, and he tries to treat them as accurately and fairly as possible. He has not written a bitter piece of propaganda. The reader senses that Plunkett wants desperately for the reader to learn how things actually were, without unfairly enhancing his own point of view.

The central fictional characters of the novel are a young couple who marry and struggle through the economic deprivations of the period, through the labor strike and through the lockout. Mary, the young wife, is a typical girl from a small village who has come up to Dublin to get a job as a household servant with an Anglo-Irish family in what was then called Kingstown, which is now Dun Loaghaire, south of Dublin. While working in this house she meets a young, able, and intelligent Irish lad named Fitz. They marry and move to a poorer, or working-class section of Dublin. It's the same milieu and the same background that O'Casey treats of in his plays *The Plough and The Stars* and *Juno and the Paycock*.

In their new neighborhood Fitz becomes active in the labor

8. A row of working class houses, Dublin.

movement and a staunch follower of Jim Larkin. Although loyal to the cause throughout the difficulties of the strike and the lockout, Fitz's adherence causes great pain because he knows that holding to his principles means loss of his minimal salary. Week after week he has to face the deprivations his principles are causing his wife and children. Mary and Fitz are reduced to bitter poverty, and Mary starts to sell off some of the furniture and pitiful belongings that have come down to her—items with more sentimental value than anything else—simply to get a bit of evaporated milk for the children.

But while Plunkett portrays the struggle of Mary and Fitz most movingly and sympathetically, he does not heighten it out of reality for sentimental purposes. Life was exactly like this in Dublin, and *Strumpet City* does a masterful job of letting us know what Dublin life was like for ordinary people in the early part of this century. It's a crowning irony in the novel that after the strike is over, after Mary and Fitz and their friends have been through such enormous difficulty, that the only avenue open to Fitz is to join the English army on the eve of World War I, to fight *for* England and the English establishment. Near the end of the novel Fitz is standing on board a troopship as it pulls away from Dublin:

> His heart was full of Mary. Each moment that passed was putting its extra little piece of world between them, each twist of the propeller carried him further and further from her. But she would have the allowance. The children would eat. the rent would be paid. In the Royal Army Service Corps he would learn to be a motor mechanic or a car driver. He would be sure of a job when he came back. If he came back. That was as would be.
> The soldier seemed lonely and leaned beside him on the rail.
> He was from Dublin too. He said,
> "Funny feeling—isn't it?"
> He was looking at the mountains that surrounded the bay. They were floating dreamily on sea and sunlight. Multi-colored.
> The two of them smoked together. The Black Lighthouse loomed up and fell behind them as the ship cleared the river at last and swung into the bay. Bells tinkled remotely. Their speed increased. Ireland slipped away behind. Before them lay England and training camps, beyond that the Continent. Foreign tongues, unfamiliar countries, shattered towns. War.

And Fitz pulls away. We never learn what ultimately happens to Fitz.

Plunkett also creates an Anglo-Irish couple, of the employer class. Mr. and Mrs. Bradshaw have a gracious and comfortable home, at which friends, often musical friends, gather frequently. The novel describes the pleasant evenings at the Bradshaws' house, where the sweet, melodic music the guests play and sing often comes from Thomas Moore's *Irish Melodies.*

But Mr. Bradshaw owns five ill-kept, though very high income-producing tenement houses. Mr. Bradshaw, as owner, has been clearly warned that the tenements are in such bad condition that they may collapse, but he does nothing to improve them; he does nothing to remedy the dangerous conditions. When the tenement houses do collapse, the bodies of seven people are dragged from the rubble. An actual event very similar to this occurred in Dublin in 1913. Plunkett, I repeat, is dealing with fact, not emotional propaganda.

Mr. Bradshaw appears to be an impenetrable, stiff, rather heartless creature, as do many Anglo-Irish men and women in literature. (The Anglo-Irish landowner in Hugh Leonard's recent play, *Da*, has the same rigid, stiff, skinny kind of way about her. And in *The Last Hurrah* the Yankee-American newspaper owner is a stiff skinflint, who eats minimal and unappetizing meals because he doesn't want to spend money on food.) Bradshaw fits that style of literary depiction of the Anglo-Irish. But Plunkett nicely balances, even softens, the indictment of Mr. Bradshaw by his portrayal of Mrs. Bradshaw. Though completely dominated by her husband and completely loyal to him, Mrs. Bradshaw has a bit of a heart, and tries in her way to be generous and helpful to Mary and Fitz. Before marriage Mary has worked in the Bradshaw's house as a servant, and leaves. Mrs. Bradshaw endeavors to do what she can for Mary. There is, of course, an element of Lady Bountiful in Mrs. Bradshaw's methods, but her motivations are sound: she wants to help another human being. While performing her good deeds, she also manages to keep her generosity a secret from her husband, because she knows her husband would forbid her to continue. Plunkett obviously wanted to balance or at least put in perspective the numerous Mr. Bradshaws who undoubtedly existed at the time.

Another powerful character in *Strumpet City*, Father O'Connor, is a young priest who is trying to come to grips with the suffering and class difference in Ireland. A friend of the well-to-do Bradshaws, Father O'Connor shows a bit of spiritual pride when he requests an assignment to a very poor parish in Dublin. He wants to help people, but he also wants to experience deprivation and thereby earn spiritual credit. For the most part he fails completely. He thinks that the strikers are motivated by an evil, corrupt desire for materialistic gain. Though he's got them right before him, the horrible conditions in which the workers live don't enter his consciousness. He also judges the labor movement to be socialistic, and he somehow *knows* the socialism is bad. Because he fears socialism, indeed is horrified by it, he can have no sympathy for the strikers whatsoever. He even refuses to give the strikers food for themselves or their children, because he thinks this will permit the evil strike to continue. He opposes strongly and works against the efforts of the labor leader, Jim Larkin, to send the hungry children to live temporarily in England. Father O'Connor fears that the English will try to wean the children from Catholicism to Protestantism. His totally distorted thinking leads Father O'Connor to physically charge into the people leading children onto the ships to go to England. His principles completely blind him to human pain and suffering. Only in the last pages of the novel, in a scene we will discuss below, may Father O'Connor's eyes be opened finally.

Plunkett balances his portrayal of Father O'Connor by depicting another priest, Father Giffley, the old and alcoholic pastor of the church that Father O'Connor is assigned to. Father Giffley has a kind of unclouded human sympathy with his poor parishioners. His alcoholism is in many ways caused by the depths of his own identification with and sympathy for the human pain that he has seen and has dealt with for several decades in Dublin. He is, of course, a flawed character, but he is a genuine human being who is loyal to his church and his beliefs, and is as dedicated to his parishioners' spiritual welfare as he is to their basic human dignity.

The character who probably speaks for Plunkett in the novel is an intelligent and sensible analyst named Belton Yearling. While he is Anglo-Irish, and a friend of the Bradshaws, he also displays much of the human empathy and sympathy of Father Giffley. Although Yearling belongs to the employer class, he also understands and sympathizes with the labor movement. He reacts with feeling to immediate events, but he also understands and gives expression to some of the central historical and social issues.

But the character who most attracts the reader's attention is a poor, old itinerant, Rashers Tierney. Rashers Tierney ekes out a living selling little flags and trinkets at parades. He also plays a tin whistle on the street, hoping for a penny from various passersby. He is the most sympathetically, the most amusingly and also the most effectively drawn character in the novel. At the very lowest level of life in Dublin, he bears the brunt of the indignity, the suffering, and the human cruelty that has resulted from the human and the political struggles between the English and the Irish; he suffers most the injustice of the class system with its enmity between workers and owners. In Tierney Plunkett presents a human being in horrible pain and dire straits because of man's quarreling inhumanity, an inhumanity mightily reminiscent of that in Swift's "Modest Proposal." Man's inhumanity to man falls very heavily on Rashers Tierney.

At the end of the book it's the body of Rashers Tierney who has died in a cellar, cold and hungry, that Father O'Connor faces with horror and with, for the first time, a certain sympathy. This fairly large section of the novel is worthy of quotation.

News of something wrong spread through Chandlers Court like a fire. A body found; a woman drunk, a suicide. By the time Father O'Connor arrived the details were known. People were spread on the pavement outside. They lined the hallway. They leaned over the basement bannisters. Down below it was dark, but neighbours had provided candles which gave a wavering light. A man found dead. This was better than the parades and the make-believe. This was the drama of death. They had passed time and again along the street above the cardboarded window. Little knowing. A woman told another that only that morning she had remarked it to her husband. She had wondered, she said. There were women with shawls, subdued children, men with grave faces.

"This way, Father," Hennessy said. He assumed a natural precedence, having been the discoverer. The people made passage.

"What exactly has happened?" Father O'Connor asked.

"I called down to see him about an hour ago. He was dead."

"Called down to see whom?" Father O'Connor asked shortly.

"Rashers Tierney," Hennessy said.

Father O'Connor stopped.

"It's not a pleasant sight, Father," Hennessy said, "he's been dead for some days."

Father O'Connor had remembered a figure in candlelight lying on a coke heap. He could smell urine and the reek of spirits. The memory was arrestingly vivid.

"Show me the way," he said, after a moment.

As he passed all their eyes were fixed on him, depending on him. For what, he did not know. It was as though they expected him to do something about Death. He shook off the lingering influence of the white cloth, the wine, the learned talk that had so transformed the common room of St. Brigid's. These were his parishioners. This was the true reality of his world. He was here of his own free choice. He had demanded to be allowed to serve them.

Led by Hennessy he passed between the candles they had set along the stairway and into the dimly lit room. The smell of corruption was overpowering. In the corner furthest from him sacking covered the body. They had decided for decency sake to hide it from him. He searched the faces of the few men in the room and recognised Fitz. He looked at the bulging sacking.

"Is that he?"

Fitz nodded.

"He's been dead for some time?"

"Several days, Father, by the look of it."

"Then there's little I can do," Father O'Connor said. He meant it was too late for the administration of the last rites but they would know that already. Presumably. They nevertheless continued to regard him. Expecting what? The smell was sweet, sickly, unbearable. He could not minister to carrion.

"Have you notified the police?"

"We have," Fitz said.

There would be an inquest. They would take it to the morgue and bury it God knows how or where. The sooner the better. In the interest of health, if nothing else.

These were the ones who refused to trust him because they thought he had tried to break their strikes when all he intended was to give a little charity to the old and the destitute. They expected him as a priest to lead a prayer for the dead boilerman. That was their right. But he would do more than that. He motioned to Hennessy.

"Remove the sacking."

They had not expected it. He saw them looking uneasily at Fitz, waiting for him to answer for them.

"He's in a very bad way, Father," Fitz said, "the rats . . ."

Delicacy stopped him from finishing. Hennessy hung back. Father O'Connor removed his hat and handed it to one of the men. He had decided what to do. He went across the room, bent down, began gently to pull down the sacking. He sweated, strangling his impulse to cry out.

The head had been savaged by rats. The nose, the ears, the checks, the eyes had been torn away. The hands had been eaten. He forced himself to be calm.

"Is this Tierney?" he asked quietly.

"It is, Father."

"And what is this?"

Hennessy came over obediently and looked. His face was a silver-grey colour.

"It's his dog, Father."

For the moment they had forgotten all about that. The animal's ribs were etched starkly against the taut skin of its carcass. Its discoloured teeth from which the lips had fallen away, wore the wide grin of death. The rats had ripped open its belly and exposed its organs.

In a voice that had found a new tone of gentleness Father O'Connor said:

"It isn't fitting to lay the brute beast and the baptised body together."

Hennessy understood. He bent down and took the dog by the forelegs, dragging it slowly across the floor and steering it into the darkness of the far corner. Father O'Connor went down on his knees. The rest knelt one by one. He took a small bottle from his pocket and, making the sign of his blessing, gravely sprinkled with holy water what decay and the rats had left of the boilerman Rashers Tierney. He prayed silently once again, aware of how often he had failed, for the grace to know how to serve without pride and without self. He prayed, as was his way, to a crown of thorns and a pair of outstretched palms, his Christ of Compassion who always looked like the statue that had once stood in Miss Gilchrist's ward.

It was some time before he remembered the others. He had excluded them from what he was about and that was wrong. Taking the mother of pearl rosary from his pocket he said:

"Let us pray together for the repose of his soul."

He began the usual decade of the rosary. At first only those in the room responded. Then to his surprise, for he had forgotten they were there, he heard the responses being taken up by those outside. The sound grew and filled the house. From those lining the stairway outside and the landing and the hallway above, voices rose and fell in rhythmical waves. The sound flowed about him, filled him, lifted him up like a great tide. He looked down at the revaged body without fear and without revulsion. Age and the rot of death were brothers, for rich and poor alike. Neither intellect nor ignorance could triumph over them. What was spread on the straw before him was no more than the common mystery, the everyday fate, the cruel heart of the world.

The prayers finished. There was one more thing to do. He did it without hesitation and without reasoning why. He joined what was left of the two half-eaten hands across the body and wrapped his mother's rosary beads about them. He pulled the sack back into position. He rose to his feet.

The man who had been minding his hat returned it to him and he put it on. There was nothing further to be done.

"God bless you all" he said to the assembled men. They made a way for him through the crowd and saw him to his cab.

Noticeable in the section is the anger combined with the compassion that Plunkett feels in this novel. A similar kind of anger and distress springs forth in Yeats' poem "September 1913," written in the month of Bloody Sunday.

In his earlier poems Yeats employed a soft, lyrical, melodic idealism. In "September 1913" disappointment, even bitterness forces Yeats to abandon his song-like melodies, with their lyrical cadence; he shifts to sharp words and a biting conversational tone as he laments the failure of past hopes for Ireland. He lays the blame on a commercial class and its shabby values and on a complacent and limited pietism. He feels quite strongly that materialism and pietism have dried up the bones at the very core of the Irish. They're not people, not the idealistic human beings that Yeats used to see them as when their roots and their values were simple, lofty, and Celtic.

In the poem Yeats cites his old Fenian friend, O'Leary, an early, somewhat fanatical, activist in the nationalist movement. To suggest the ideals and hopes of the past, Yeats calls up earlier heroes like Wolfe Tone, Lord Edward Fitzgerald, and Robert Emmett, who was hanged, drawn, and quartered in 1803 for supporting a rebellion. Their heroism contrasts with his view of contemporary Ireland and its grubbing materialism.

What need you, being come to sense,
But fumble in a greasy till
And add the halfpence to pence
And prayer to shivering prayer, until
You have dried the marrow from the bone?
For men were born to pray and save:

Romantic Ireland's dead and gone,
It's with O'Leary in the grave.

Yet they were of a different kind,
The names that stilled your childish play,
They have gone about the world like wind,
But little time had they to pray
For whom the hangman's rope was spun,
And what, God help us, could they save?
Romantic Ireland's dead and gone,
It's with O'Leary in the grave.

Was it for this the wild geese spread
The grey wing upon every tide;
For this that all that blood was shed,
For this Edward Fitzgerald died,
And Robert Emmet and Wolfe Tone,
All that delirium of the brave?
Romantic Ireland's dead and gone,
It's with O'Leary in the grave.

Yet could we turn the years again,
And call those exiles as they were
In all their loneliness and pain,
You'd cry, "Some woman's yellow hair
Has maddened every mother's son":
They weighed so lightly what they gave.
But let them be, they're dead and gone,
They're with O'Leary in the grave.

The last stanza contains an apparent reference to Yeats' own "Cathleen ni Houlihan," the line "Some woman's yellow hair has maddened every mother's son." Cathleen did, in a sense, madden and lure Michael Gillane from his cottage and into the 1798 Rebellion. Yeats bitterly contrasts the giving of self for Ireland in the past with the sordid present, when Irishmen care only about fumbling in the greasy till and adding the halfpence to the pence. Believing Ireland was being corrupted by a commercial class, by the middle class, Yeats lamented the loss of what he saw as the more idealistic and imaginative old Celtic values.

Another Yeats poem from this same period, "To A Shade," speaks of Parnell as representing the old dream for Ireland, the dream that sparked the literary movement, so vibrant at the turn of the century. By 1913 the old hopes for making the idealized Ireland a reality had gone completely. Distress was the reality of contemporary Dublin.

In "To A Shade" Yeats focuses on William Martin Murphy, called "an old foul mouth." You will recall from *Strumpet City* that Murphy was the leader of the employers who decided to break the strike in Dublin by locking out the workers. Yeats had a particular hatred for William Martin Murphy, not only because of the lockout but also because Murphy had offended a friend of his, Hugh Lane, a Dubliner related to Lady Gregory, a close friend of Yeats. Lane had shrewdly and carefully collected a large group of paintings, particularly French impressionist paintings. He hoped to bring an element of culture to Ireland by giving the collection of the paintings to the City of Dublin. He stipulated that he would give Dublin the paintings if it provided the building to house them. William Martin Murphy opposed Hugh Lane's proposal when it came for decision before the city government, and the Hugh Lane's offer was refused. From Yeats' point of view this act showed yet again that the growing commercial class, the group William Martin Murphy represented, had no understanding of culture, nor of cultural values, in the life of a city or a nation. Moreover William Martin Murphy had led the attack against Parnell at the meeting to decide whether Parnell should continue as chairman of the National League after the revelation of his scandalous affair with Kitty O'Shea. So Yeats had plenty of reason to detest William Martin Murphy; but he doesn't mention him by name, rather he calls him an old foul-mouth.

This poem reveals how Parnell's downfall energized the nationalist movement in Ireland and how his image remained as a reference point for writers. Yeats talks not merely about Parnell's spirit, or shade, but about Parnell's grave in Glasnevin cemetery.

Notice how just as in "September 1913" Yeats uses a conversational idiom, the word order of ordinary speech, rather than one which produces a melodic cadence.

If you have revisited the town, thin Shade,
Whether to look upon the monument
(I wonder if the builder has been paid)
Or happier-thoughted when the day is spent
To drink of that salt breath out of the sea
When grey gulls flit about instead of men,

And the gaunt houses put on majesty:
Let these content you and be gone again;
For they are at their old tricks yet.

Of your own passionate serving kind A man who had brought
In his full hands what, had they only known,
Had given their children's children loftier thought,
Sweeter emotion, working in their veins
Like gentle blood, has been driven from the place,
And insult heaped upon him for his pains,
And for his open-handedness, disgrace;
Your enemy, an old foul mouth, had set
The pack upon him.

Go, unquiet wanderer,
And gather the Glasnevin coverlet
About your head till the dust stops your ear,
The time for you to taste of that salt breath
And listen at the corners has not come;
You had enough of sorrow before death—
Away, away! You are safer in the tomb.

In the lamentation of the poem, notice that the hopes of
Parnell for Ireland are combined with the sea with its gulls and its
salt air. These hopes have been dashed by William Martin Murphy
and his way of life. Here again, as in "September 1913" and in
Strumpet City, we find tremendous anger and intense bitterness.
And in that anger and bitterness we can foresee the eruption of the
Easter Rebellion of 1916.

CHAPTER SIX

1916 Rebellion

ONE OF THE first things we notice about the Easter Rebellion of 1916 is that among its leaders were idealistic poets and school teachers. Earlier I mentioned that the literary figures in the twentieth century tend to move history rather than respond to it; the poets who led the 1916 Rebellion certainly illustrate this. One significant leader of that insurgence was Patrick Pearse, who was both a school teacher and a poet.

Others who helped lead the Rebellion included men like James Connolly, who wanted to improve the economic life of the ordinary people of Ireland. Fired as it was by idealistic motivations rather than by arms and well-planned military strategy, the Rebellion failed partially as a consequence of tactical weakness. But the leader of the Rebellion, Patrick Pearse, was strong in purpose, strong in idealism, and strong in his desire for Ireland's freedom. The strength of his purpose and his idealism are clearly evident in the poetry he wrote at that time.

Two Pearse poems remind us of Yeats' poems "To A Shade" and "September 1913," and their intense idealism recalls Yeats' play, *Cathleen ni Houlihan.*

The first poem, "The Rebel," calls upon the people of Ireland to rise up together from their long bondage. Since they are a people with vision, with soul, if they rise up together, the Rebellion will succeed. A powerful line in the poem, "Beware, beware of the thing that is coming," of course harkens toward the 1916 Rebellion. The poem calls to arms with a militancy and a zeal inspired by generations of injustice.

I am come of the seed of the people, the people that sorrow,
That have no treasure but hope,
No riches laid up but a memory
Of an ancient glory.
My mother bore me in bondage, in bondage my mother was born,
I am the blood of serfs;
The children with whom I have played, the men and women with
   whom I have eaten,
Have had masters over them, they have been under the lash of
   masters,
And, though gentle, have served churls;
The hands that have touched mine, the dear hands whose touch is
   familiar to me,
Have worn shameful manacles, have been bitten at the wrist by
   manacles,
Have grown hard with the manacles and the task-work of strangers,
I am flesh of the flesh of these lowly, I am bone of their bone,
I that have never submitted;
I that have a soul greater than the souls of my people's masters,
I that have vision and prophecy and the gift of fiery speech,
I that have spoken with God on the top of His holy hill.
And because I am of the people, I understand the people,
I am sorrowful with their sorrow, I am hungry with their desire:
My heart has been heavy with the grief of mothers,
My eyes have been wet with the tears of children,
I have yearned with old wistful men,
And laughed or cursed with young men;
Their shame is my shame, and I have reddened for it,
Reddened for that they have gone in want, while others have been
   full,
Reddened for that they have walked in fear of lawyers and of their
   jailors
With their writs of summons and their handcuffs,
Men mean and cruel!
I could have borne stripes on my body rather than this shame of
   my people.
And now I speak, being full of vision;
I speak to my people, and I speak in my people's name to the
masters of my people.
I say to my people that they are holy, that they are august,
   despite their chains,
That they are greater than those that hold them, and stronger
   and purer,

That they have but need of courage, and to call on the name of
   their God,
God the unforgetting, the dear God that loves the peoples
For whom He died naked, suffering shame.
And I say to my people's masters: Beware,
Beware of the thing that is coming, beware of the risen people,
Who shall take what ye would not give. Did ye think to conquer
   the people,
Or that Law is stronger than life and than men's desire to
   be free?
We will try it out with you, ye that have harried and held,
Ye that have bullied and bribed, tyrants, hypocrites!

The speaker in "The Fool" is one of the people who refused to
be conquered. Because the speaker believes in his dream, "A dream
that was dreamed in the heart and only the heart could hold," he is
called a fool. But notice the line, "What if the dream come true?"
The goal of the rebels is, of course, to make their dream come true.
Compare "What if the dream come true" with similar statements by
Martin Luther King during the Black movement in the United
States in the sixties, lines such as the frequently quoted "I have a
dream." Patrick Pearse's dream is similar; he calls for the people to
make the impossible come true by banding together.

Since the wise men have not spoken, I speak that am only a fool;
A fool that hath loved his folly,
Yea, more than the wise men their books or their counting
   house, or their quiet homes,
Or their fame in men's mouths;
A fool that in all his days hath done never a prudent thing,
Never hath counted the cost, nor recked if another reaped
The fruit of his mighty sowing, content to scatter the seed;
A fool that is unrepentant, and that soon at the end of all
Shall laugh in his lonely heart as the ripe ears fall to the
   reaping-hooks
And the poor are filled that were empty,
Tho' he go hungry.

I have squandered the splendid years that the Lord God gave to
   my youth
In attempting impossible things, deeming them alone worth the toil.
Was it folly or grace? Not men shall judge me, but God.

I have squandered the splendid years:
Lord, if I had the years I would squander them over again,
Aye, fling them from me!
For this I have heard in my heart, that a man shall scatter,
     not hoard,
Shall do the deed of to-day, nor take thought of to-morrow's teen,
Shall not bargain or huxter with God; or was it a jest of Christ's
And is this my sin before men, to have taken Him at His word?

The lawyers have sat in council, the men with the keen,
     long faces,
And said, "This man is a fool," and others have said, "He
     blasphemeth;"
And the wise have pitied the fool that hath striven to give a life
In the world of time and space among the bulks of actual things,
To a dream that was dreamed in the heart, and that only
     the heart could hold.

O wise men, riddle me this: what if the dream come true?
What if the dream come true? and if millions unborn shall dwell
In the house that I shaped in my heart, the noble house of
     my thought?
Lord, I have staked my soul, I have staked the lives of my kin
On the truth of Thy dreadful word. Do not remember my failures,
But remember this my faith.

And so I speak.
Yea, ere my hot youth pass, I speak to my people and say:
Ye shall be foolish as I; ye shall scatter, not save;
Ye shall venture your all, lest ye lose what is more than all;
Ye shall call for a miracle, taking Christ at His word.
And for this I will answer, O people, answer here and hereafter,
O people that I have loved, shall we not answer together?

Patrick Pearse and his followers tried to make their dream
come true. On Easter Monday of 1916, from the steps of the General
Post Office on what is now O'Connell Street in Dublin, they read
The Proclamation for the Irish Republic. Their idealism was so
strong that they believed if they proclaimed a free Irish Republic,
then the Irish would automatically see the truth and rise up
together; they would know the truth and the truth would set them
free. There's something a bit naive in that assumption, for many
Irish in Dublin didn't understand, as they went about their business,

POBLACHT NA H EIREANN.

THE PROVISIONAL GOVERNMENT
OF THE
IRISH REPUBLIC
TO THE PEOPLE OF IRELAND.

IRISHMEN AND IRISHWOMEN : In the name of God and of the dead generations from which she receives her old tradition of nationhood, Ireland, through us, summons her children to her flag and strikes for her freedom.

Having organised and trained her manhood through her secret revolutionary organisation, the Irish Republican Brotherhood, and through her open military organisations, the Irish Volunteers and the Irish Citizen Army, having patiently perfected her discipline, having resolutely waited for the right moment to reveal itself, she now seizes that moment, and, supported by her exiled children in America and by gallant allies in Europe, but relying in the first on her own strength, she strikes in full confidence of victory.

We declare the right of the people of Ireland to the ownership of Ireland, and to the unfettered control of Irish destinies, to be sovereign and indefeasible. The long usurpation of that right by a foreign people and government has not extinguished the right, nor can it ever be extinguished except by the destruction of the Irish people. In every generation the Irish people have asserted their right to national freedom and sovereignty: six times during the past three hundred years they have asserted it in arms. Standing on that fundamental right and again asserting it in arms in the face of the world, we hereby proclaim the Irish Republic as a Sovereign Independent State, and we pledge our lives and the lives of our comrades-in-arms to the cause of its freedom, of its welfare, and of its exaltation among the nations.

The Irish Republic is entitled to, and hereby claims, the allegiance of every Irishman and Irishwoman. The Republic guarantees religious and civil liberty, equal rights and equal opportunities to all its citizens, and declares its resolve to pursue the happiness and prosperity of the whole nation and of all its parts, cherishing all the children of the nation equally, and oblivious of the differences carefully fostered by an alien government, which have divided a minority from the majority in the past.

Until our arms have brought the opportune moment for the establishment of a permanent National Government, representative of the whole people of Ireland and elected by the suffrages of all her men and women, the Provisional Government, hereby constituted, will administer the civil and military affairs of the Republic in trust for the people.

We place the cause of the Irish Republic under the protection of the Most High God, Whose blessing we invoke upon our arms, and we pray that no one who serves that cause will dishonour it by cowardice, inhumanity, or rapine. In this supreme hour the Irish nation must, by its valour and discipline and by the readiness of its children to sacrifice themselves for the common good, prove itself worthy of the august destiny to which it is called.

Signed on Behalf of the Provisional Government,

THOMAS J. CLARKE.
SEAN Mac DIARMADA.   THOMAS MacDONAGH.
P. H. PEARSE,   EAMONN CEANNT,
JAMES CONNOLLY.   JOSEPH PLUNKETT.

9. The Proclamation of the Irish Republic announced at the Easter Rising, (National Museum of Ireland)

10. The leaders of the Easter Rising executed in 1916. Patrick Pearse, center; Thomas Clarke, top; and clockwise, Thomas MacDonagh, James Connolly, Sean MacDiarmada, Joseph Mary Plunkett, Eamon Ceannt. Also executed was John McBride. (National Museum of Ireland)

what Pearse and his followers were doing on the Post Office steps that day.

The proclamation says in part:

> The Provisional Government of the Irish Republic to the People of Ireland.
>
> Irishmen and Irishwomen: In the name of God and of the dead generations from which she receives her old tradition of nationhood, Ireland, through us, summons her children to her flag and strikes for her freedom. . . .
>
> We declare the right of the people of Ireland to the ownership of Ireland, and to the unfettered control of Irish destinies, to be sovereign and indefeasible. The long usurpation of that right by a foreign people and government has not extinguished the right, nor can it ever be extinguished except by the destruction of the Irish people. In every generation the Irish people have asserted their right to national freedom and sovereignty; six times during the past three hundred years they have asserted it in arms. Standing on that fundamental right and again asserting it in arms in the face of the world, we hereby proclaim the Irish Republic as a Sovereign Independent State, and we pledge our lives and the lives of our comrades-in-arms to the cause of its freedom, of its welfare, and of its exultation among the nations.

After the Proclamation was read that Easter Monday, skirmishes and fighting broke out in various parts of Dublin. The leaders of the Rebellion had stationed groups of slightly trained soldiers at major roadways in the hope that they could prevent the British from bringing in reinforcements. The rebellion began on a day when an important horse race was being run on the outskirts of Dublin, so most of the English from Dublin Castle were at the horse race. Fighting occurred in various parts of Dublin, much of it on O'Connell Street, but in a few days the British forces contained and overwhelmed the rebels. After the rebel leaders surrendered, they were taken to Kilmainham Jail, now a chillingly effective museum. The leaders were quickly tried and shot in front of the gray walls of the prison. One leader, James Connolly, had been seriously wounded in the fighting, but the British had him carted to the wall in a wheelbarrow and tied him upright in a chair to face the firing squad. The Irish have never forgotten how Connolly was executed. Many still claim that their grandfather was one of the men who helped wheel him out. Of course there can't be all that many who did, but James Connolly lives on to inspire some present-day organizations.

Also executed was Patrick Pearse, the dedication in his poems fully validated by his commitment to the rebellion and by his death.

One of the ironies of the day was that while the rebel leaders expected Dubliners to rise in support of the Rebellion, many of the Dublin poor — not understanding or even knowing what was going on — decided to use the disturbances to help themselves to all the things in store windows that they hadn't been able to buy. Considerable looting took place throughout Dublin, a detail Sean O'Casey picks up on in "The Plough and the Stars." He points out the great disparity between the idealistic zeal of the Rebellion leaders and the understanding and immediate needs of ordinary Dubliners.

The Rebellion, obviously, had failed. And although the Abbey Theatre immediately commemorated the executions of the leaders with a production of "Cathleen ni Houlihan," the idealism of the leaders had certainly met in head-on collision with the realities of military strength and actual power.

After 1916, Irish literature tends to be much less idealistic and considerably more realistic, often even cynical. The lyrical dreams and rhythmic evocations of an idealized, romanticized Ireland give way to bitter, somewhat grim presentations of reality. Cynicism and bitterness pervade James Joyce. Negativism characterizes the present-day writer John McGahern. And certainly we can see it immediately in Sean O'Casey's "The Plough and the Stars."

In the play we see O'Casey's distress with the real suffering and bloodshed caused by the 1916 Rebellion, for which he held Patrick Pearse and his followers responsible. He believed them totally unworldly and indicted their lack of awareness about the real world of hurt and loss of life, the world inhabited by the poor and the ordinary people.

O'Casey himself had been raised in the poverty of Dublin, had experienced and seen the city's widespread distress. For O'Casey it was that distress, that reality, which needed dramatic articulation. He preferred to shift away from the idealized peasant play, from the idealized peasant cottage, from "Cathleen ni Houlihan," and move to the miseries of Dublin's tenements and slums. He succeeds in "The Plough and the Stars."

The opening act of the play is set in the crowded living room of

11. Sean O'Casey's portrait by Augustus John. [Metropolitan Museum of Art, Bequest of Stephen Clark, 1960. (61.101.9)]

a Dublin tenement. Because there are numerous people, many actions are going on simultaneously. No one character is quite listening to any other character; no one is responding or paying attention to anyone else. Meanwhile outside the window a parade of Irish patriots marches by. A good deal of the play depends upon comparison between the actions going on inside the house and the actions going on outside the house. Those outside reflect the militant idealism of Patrick Pearse, while those inside chronicle the every day, the groping of the tenement dwellers for their marginal existence. The outside idealistic action is remote from and contrasts dramatically with the inside realistic action.

Gradually the people inside the house become aware of the parade outside. A bricklayer named Jack Clitheroe and his wife Nora have only recently married. Jack craves glory and wants to join the Irish patriots for the sole purpose of becoming a hero. In many ways he doesn't understand the Rebellion. He simply perceives it as an opportunity for him to become important. His wife Nora pleads with him not to join the army, for she wants a real, live husband, not a dead hero.

O'Casey presents the same triangle that Yeats did in "Cathleen ni Houlihan." In that play the groom-to-be is lured away on the night before his marriage by the symbolic embodiment of the Irish nation, Cathleen ni Houlihan. For Yeats the proper choice was to go off and fight and die for Ireland in the 1798 Rebellion. For O'Casey, however, Jack makes the wrong decision when he goes to fight in the 1916 Rebellion. To join the Citizens Army and fight means that he's leaving his life and home responsibilities and causing difficulties for another human being, his wife. The triangle is the same in both plays; the attitudes of the authors are diametrically opposed. Act One of *The Plough and the Stars* closes as Jack chooses country, or more accurately potential glory, over wife, and leaving Nora crying, marches out to join the Citizens Army.

Act Two, the play's best and most masterful, takes place inside a pub in Dublin. As the curtain opens one of the customers in the pub is a prostitute, Rosie. To portray a prostitute on the stage in Dublin was a bit of shocking realism for the Irish at the time. Rosie claims she's having a very hard time making a living in Dublin, not because she lacks Irish customers, but simply because her rent's going up. As she complains, the voice of Patrick Pearse comes in from outside the window — again the action inside contrasts with the action outside. O'Casey has carefully, maybe unfairly, selected some of Pearse's most sabre-rattling speeches saying how noble it is to die for Ireland. The outside idealisms, now explicitly those of Patrick Pearse, contrast with the earthy vitality inside the pub, in this case the economic problems of a whore. O'Casey prefers life inside the pub to life outside.

Rosie sidles up to a customer at the bar, Fluther, whom we know from the tenement in Act One. He decides to take her up, and the two of them leave. As they go out the door, a soldier enters, carrying the Irish flag, the tricolor. The scene is basically exit whore, enter flag. At this point in the first Dublin production the audience became so outraged that they rioted in the theater, claiming offense to their notions of Ireland and the Irish. Of course the irony of the contrast between the reality of the pub and the hardened zeal of the nationalist movement is absolutely fierce, and O'Casey very clearly casts himself on the side of the vitality of the pub life and clearly condemns the idealisms of the nationalist movement of 1916.

The third acts shifts from the pub to the streets. The poor scurry about looting the stores, for the Rebellion has given them a chance to grab some of the things they've been denied by their poverty or by the injustices that had gone on for decades or for centuries. The poor have O'Casey's complete understanding and sympathy. For him life exists in the individual, not in any kind of ideological construct, any "ism,"—the kind of ism, ideal or national, that led to the 1916 Rebellion and its bloodshed.

In this act Nora sees her husband Jack and renews and intensifies her pleas, knowing that if he goes to the barricades he will be killed. They argue and Jack, in anger and in strong desire to be a hero, throws Nora to the floor and stomps out to the barricades and his death. As he marches away at the close of the act, the audience learns that Nora is pregnant.

The fourth and final act further dramatizes, perhaps over dramatizes, O'Casey's contention that causes do nothing but hurt the people at the bottom. In the act a young tenement child named Mollser, who has been coughing intermittently in previous acts, dies from tuberculosis, a fearful and widespread disease at the time. And the audience learns that Nora has miscarried her baby primarily because her husband's death and her consequent impoverishment and loneliness have driven her mad. She appears pathetically pale, in a night dress, with her hair hanging down, not quite realizing

12. Abbey Theatre actors portraying characters in a Sean O'Casey play. (Irish Tourist Board)

where she is. She has been totally defeated by Cathleen ni Houlihan, and O'Casey stops at nothing to win sympathy for her. For many O'Casey goes too far; the last act borders on soap opera with its abundant accumulation of miseries. But others think that this act reflects accurately the reality of Dublin at the time.

As Nora wanders about in this half-crazed and disheveled state, a neighbor, a strong woman named Bessie Burgess, appears. Here is O'Casey's heroine, the person he most admires. Bessie is crude, vulgar, and very human. O'Casey has given Bessie the kind of elemental energy, vitality, and zest that he admires, a zest that O'Casey believes decreases if people become prosperous, get overly educated, overly sophisticated, or somehow or other elegant. The higher the class, for O'Casey, the lower the zest the people have for life.

Anti-materialism—that frequent Irish theme—recurs here. The more things one owns, the more money one possesses, the less life, the less feeling, the less heart one has. For O'Casey, energy and elegance are opposites. He continually praises energy, endurance, suffering, and a basic humanity. Tough and brawling Bessie Burgess has vitality and a great big wonderful heart, far more important qualities for O'Casey than the abstract goals of the 1916 Rebellion.

Near the end of the act, Nora, in her crazed condition, foolishly wanders by a window. Again, notice the repetition of a cruel action outside, for as Nora walks by the window, a sniper takes her for a target. Bessie Burgess instinctively lunges forward to hurl Nora to the floor to prevent her from being killed, but in so doing, Bessie herself is shot. Bessie Burgess does not die the usual heroic enobled death, marked with moving last words. She dies sputtering coarsely, berating Nora for being so dumb as to walk in front of the window. As she is shot, she jerks convulsively and suddenly, astonished, recognizes what has happened. She then screams a little and says:

"Merciful God, I'm shot, I'm shot, I'm shot! . . .
Th' life's pourin' out o' me! (To Nora)
I've got this through . . . through you . . . through you, you
bitch, you! . . . O God, have mercy on me! . . . (To Nora)
You wouldn't stop quiet, no, you wouldn't, you wouldn't, blast you!
Look at what I'm afther gettin', look at what I'm afther gettin' . . .

I'm bleedin' to death, an' no one's here to stop
th' flowin' blood! . . . for God's sake, somebody,
a doctor, a doctor!"

Nora merely wanders around, not really knowing what's going
on, whimpering,

"Oh, Jack, where are you?"

Bessie continus to moan:

"This is what's afther comin' on me for nursin' you day an' night . . .
I was a fool, a fool, a fool!
Get me a dhrink o' wather, you jade, will you?
There's a fire burnin' in me blood! . . .
Nora, Nora, dear, for God's sake,
run out an' get . . . somebody to bring a doctor quick, quick,
quick! . . . Blast you, stir yourself, before I'm gone! . . .
Jesus Christ, me sight's goin'! It's all dark, dark!
Nora, hold me hand! . . . I'm dyin', I'm dyin' . . . I feel it . . .
   Oh God, Oh God!"

And then she feebly sings a little song:

"I do believe, I will believe
   That Jesus died for me;
That on th' cross He shed His blood,
   From sin to set me free. . . .
I do believe . . . I will believe
   . . . Jesus died . . . me.

And then she dies. Her sputtering energy as she curses Nora shows
she's still tough, even at death. For O'Casey, that's the way it should
be; the more vibrant, the more brawling, the more gutsy, the better.

After Bessie dies, some ordinary English soldiers come in, sit
down, and have some tea. While they're having their tea, they sing,
"Keep The Home Fires Burning" in cockney accents, ending the
play with bitter and biting irony.

What O'Casey has done in the play is celebrate life, condemn-
ing anything that lessens life and its energies. For O'Casey, the effects of the Rebellion are painfully clear: it has done nothing but

cause the kind of hurt, suffering, and death we have seen before us. The Cause of Freedom has gained no one anything. For O'Casey, a confident and consistent pacifist, no cause deserves the loss of a drop of blood. Even in World War II O'Casey remained a pacifist.

The 1916 Rebellion was of course a clash between the Irish and the English, but it also was, as I said, a deeper clash between idealism and reality. And I suggest that 1916 changed Irish literature. The one writer of the 1916 Rebellion who clearly saw, understood, and sympathized with both sides at the same time—with the idealism of a Pearse, and the realism of an O'Casey—was William Butler Yeats. We can see his ambivalence in "Easter 1916," where he shows clearly the full tragedy of the deaths yet the admirable heroism of the leaders.

You will remember that in his "September 1913," written at the time of the Dublin lockout, Yeats castigated the Irish for becoming increasingly corrupted by materialism; people cared only about putting money in "the greasy till." Yeats' dissatisfaction continued into 1916, when to his amazement the Rebellion occurred. The heroic capacities of the leaders shook him out of his distress and inspired a new admiration which "Easter 1916" dramatically expresses. The opening lines recall what he's come to think of the Irish—as boring people in routine existences.

> I have met with them at close of day
> Coming with vivid faces
> From counter or desk among grey
> Eighteenth-century houses.
> I have passed with a nod of the head
> Or polite meaningless words,
> Or have lingered awhile and said
> Polite meaningless words,
> And thought before I had done
> Of a mocking tale or a gibe
> To please a companion
> Around the fire at the club,
> Being certain that they and I
> But lived where motley is worn:
> All changed, changed utterly.
> A terrible beauty is born.

The last lines expose Yeats' ambivalence. There's admiration for the beauty and heroism of the Rebellion and simultaneous horror at its terror and loss of life. In the next stanza Yeats sketches some of the leaders of the Rebellion who have been executed or imprisoned. The first, referring to Countess Marciewicz:

> That woman's days were spent
> In ignorant good-will,
> Her nights in argument
> Until her voice grew shrill.
> What voice more sweet that hers
> When young and beautiful,
> She rode to harriers?

For Patrick Pearse:

> This man had kept a school
> And rode our wingèd horse

For the poet Thomas McDonagh:

> This other his helper and friend
> Was coming into his force;
> He might have won fame in the end,
> So sensitive his nature seemed,
> So daring and sweet his thought.

For John McBride, whom Yeats disliked heartily because he married Maude Gonne, the woman that Yeats wanted to marry:

> This other man I had dreamed
> A drunken, vainglorious lout.
> He had done most bitter wrong
> To some who are near my heart,
> Yet I number him in the song;
> He, too, has resigned his part
> In the casual comedy;
> He, too, has been changed in his turn,
> Transformed utterly:
> A terrible beauty is born.

One senses Yeats' amazement that the people he thought were vainglorious louts or usual individuals had been startingly transformed into heroes.

The next stanza is more difficult. Yeats shifts to a new image, pointing out that an overzealous singleness of purpose narrows the breadth of anyone's perspective. If one has a single cause and cares strongly about it, he loses any possible sense of awareness of other matters. When that happens, part of the person's life is diminished since he cares about only one thing, when there are so many others possible in addition. Hence, when a heart gets one purpose, the heart is hardened so that the flow of blood is somewhat narrowed or stopped. The person is not as alive as he might be if he had retained a broader perspective. Hence, the lines:

> Hearts with one purpose alone
> Through summer and winter seem
> Enchanted to a stone
> To trouble the living stream.

Yeats then takes up that picture of the living stream.

> The horse that comes from the road,
> The rider, the birds that range
> From cloud to tumbling cloud,
> Minute by minute they change;
> A shadow of cloud on the stream
> Changes minute by minute;
> A horse-hoof slides on the brim,
> And a horse plashes within it;
> The long-legged moor-hens dive,
> And hens to moor-cocks call;
> Minute by minute they live:
> The stone's in the midst of all.

The hard stone in the stream "troubles" the living stream, as the hardened heart troubles the living blood stream. Life continues but the hardened stone squats in the middle of it. The comparison that follows shows that the hearts of the Rebellion's leaders became so fanatical that they really stopped their own lives, or caused their own deaths. Their singularity of purpose prevented their seeing beyond it. Eventually the purpose caused their deaths, the sacrifice of themselves. While life continues to go on, they happen to be dead. So they are, in a sense, the stone in the midst of all.

The next lines raise a question that follows from that sacrifice:

Too long a sacrifice
Can make a stone of the heart.
O when may it suffice?

When *is* a cause worth the loss of a life? At what point can any
human being say that he is willing to lay down his life for some particular cause? For the leaders of the 1916 Rebellion, the 1916
Rebellion was cause enough. For Yeats the question remains
unanswerable.

That is Heaven's part, our part
To murmur name upon name,
As a mother names her child
When sleep at last has come
On limbs that had run wild.
What is it but nightfall?
No. no, not night but death;
Was it needless death after all?
For England may keep faith
For all that is done and said.

England had promised Ireland Home Rule, but World War I
delayed it. At the time he wrote the poem Yeats speculated that
England might grant Home Rule without further rebellion. Was it
then needless for the leaders to stage that Rebellion at all (although
Home Rule would not have sufficed for Pearse, who wanted total
separation)? For Yeats that too remains a question:

We know their dream; enough
To know they dreamed and are dead.

Notice that Yeats sees quite clearly both sides of the issues we've
developed here: their dream and their death. He understands the
idealism of their dream. He also understands the reality of their
death. His sympathy is on both sides. With this ambivalence he concludes in the manner of Gaelic verse, calling up in praise the list of
heroes:

And what if excess of love
Bewildered them till they died?
I write it out in a verse—

MacDonagh and MacBride
And Connolly and Pearse
Now and in time to be,
Wherever green is worn,
Are changed, changed utterly:
A terrible beauty is born.

The wording itself in the last two lines reflects Yeats' ambivalence: the symmetrical balance on each side of the comma in
the second to last line, with the word changed in each half, and the
juxtaposition of "terrible" and "beauty" in the last line.

The reader can see that Yeats understands 1916 in a dual
fashion and that he lifts the realities of the Rebellion beyond the
pathos with which O'Casey presents them, to the level of tragedy.

The execution of the leaders of the Rebellion did more to unite
the Irish in opposition to England than the Rebellion itself. Some
historians feel the English made a tactical mistake because the Irish
were so stirred by the cruelty of the executions. In a sense while the
Rebellion itself did not succeed, the executions did, perhaps as
Pearse had intended. In 1921, finally, the Irish Free State was
created. Ulster remained separate, and England retained the free
use of Irish ports for her Navy, a provision recalling the continuing
military and strategic importance of Ireland to England. These
terms did not satisfy all of the Irish, so in 1937 after many difficult
years, the Irish Free State was dissolved and the Irish Republic
created. England no longer had free use of Irish ports, but the line
of separation between Ulster and the Irish Republic continued.
There are still many today, however, who would like to obliterate
that line to make Ireland a single nation once again.

At the time of World War II Ireland determined to remain
neutral rather than to support the English and the Allies. While
many found that lamentable, history makes it understandable — after centuries of struggle Ireland could not join with
England in a war.

In the 1940s and early 1950s, Ireland turned in upon itself to
establish its independence, its own identity. Foreign investors were
not encouraged to come into Ireland, for the country wanted to
develop on its own and at its own rate. It was a circumscribed, difficult time for writers in Ireland.

In the mid fifties, however, Ireland joined the United Nations, where it actively participates in U.N. peacekeeping forces. Ireland has also joined the European economic community, has lowered the barriers to foreign investment, and is now developing rapidly. A great number of Germans have made many investments; they are, for instance taking peat or turf and compressing it into bricquets the size of ordinary bricks. These make wonderful fuel for fires, and are cheap compared to costly petroleum fuels. They are also cleaner and neater than the original turf. Japanese investors have opened textile mills in various parts of Ireland, including near the locale of "Cathleen ni Houlihan." Quite a change; such a development unsettles the old ways.

With Ireland undergoing such rapid change, the old Ireland may very well be disappearing, as writers have feared before. Back on 1800 Maria Edgeworth worried that the new union of Great Britain and Ireland might cause the distinctive Irish ways to fade away and she determined to capture the Irish flavor in her novel before it vanished. In 1907 John Synge worried that the wild country life of Ireland would be disappearing or, as he said, that the straw would be turned to brick. Right now the straw is indeed turning to brick in Ireland. The new economic developments are introducing an industrialism and materialism in many ways alien to Ireland's deeply ingrained values. Such changes will cause considerable turmoil in Irish life and in the Irish conscience, and this turmoil will, I assume, find its way into literature.

13. Bringing fuel from the land: turf cutting in the bog. (Irish Tourist Board)

CHAPTER SEVEN

Dreams and Idylls: Yeats' Early Poetry

WE NOW TURN from history and the literature entwined with history to literature that reveals and reflects the life of the Irish countryside. I am not alone in suggesting that Ireland consists of two parts—Dublin and everything else. (Of course that statement offends anyone from Cork City.) When people who have never been to Ireland ask my advice, I often suggest that they tour Ireland first and *then* go to Dublin. The clearer understanding of the country that Dublin represents as its capital city enhances appreciation for the city.

We have already gathered a notion of rural Ireland as divided into small agrarian plots farmed in elementary simplicity. But we can gain insights into country life beyond this if we turn to the literature.

The early poems of Yeats, an appropriate place to start, are closely associated with particular places in the Irish countryside. One feature which distinguishes much of Irish literature, and which certainly distinguishes Irish poetry, is the sense of place it conveys, that is, the author will talk about a certain town, a certain waterfall, a certain tree. Irish poetry has a more distinctively rich sense of place than, say, English poetry. England has, of course, been richer than Ireland in cultural *artifacts* appropriate for a poet to use as poetic symbol. For instance, when Keats writes about the passage of time and death in his famous poem "Ode on a Grecian Urn," he uses a Grecian urn such as in the British Museum as a symbol and as the fulcrum for his discussion. But life in Ireland had not encouraged collections of cultural objects such as those in the British Museum. If an Irish poet wanted to write about time, life, or some emotional or intellectual abstraction, he often used the tree outside the door of

14. Ben Bulben, mountain in County Sligo near Yeats' grandparents' home and near his selected gravesite. (Irish Tourist Board)

15. A bog in County Galway with turf neatly cut and stacked. Sky and shifting clouds dominate the landscape. (Irish Tourist Board)

the cottage, or the mountain down the road, or a particular waterfall near by.

While Yeats was born in Dublin, he spent a good deal of time in
County Sligo, the home of his grandparents. County Sligo became
his spiritual home ground. His poetry, especially his early poetry,
alludes to places and things in that particular part of Ireland. It
focuses on the beauty of the natural landscape of the west. As I suggested earlier, many of the Irish consider the west of Ireland the real
Ireland. Because it's poor, because it's remote, because the Irish
were pushed into the west of Ireland by various English incursions,
many think it is therefore more authentically Irish than other parts
of the country.

The beautiful Irish countryside provokes a highly romantic
response, a response that assumes that the Irish peasantry who lived
close to the soil were able to preserve their Celtic imagination, an
imagination that lived in close harmony with the spirits they felt inhabited the very places that they lived in, say the mountain of
Knocknarea or the mountain of Ben Bulben. For Yeats, the landscape of Sligo abounded with spirits. He believed that they were
hovering there, that they were present in the soil, and that the
peasantry lived with this spirit dimension as part of their world, seeing not only the landscape around them but the spirits who inhabited it. Yeats says this rather directly in his early poetry and
prose, particularly in a paragraph from a small collection of essays
he called *The Celtic Twilight*. In his early years, when he was tremendously enthusiastic about the Irish peasantry and the Irish landscape, Yeats wandered the byways of Sligo talking with various
country people and gathering little stories, folk stories, told by the
peasants themselves. One paragraph in the book containing these
stories, *The Celtic Twilight*, is called, "Concerning the Nearness
Together of Heaven, Earth, and Purgatory":

> In Ireland this world and the world we go to after death are not
> far apart. I have heard of a ghost that was many years in a tree
> and many years in the archway of a bridge, and my old Mayo
> woman says, "There is a bush up at my own place, and the people
> do be saying that there are two souls doing their penance under it.
> When the wind blows one way the one has shelter, and when it blows
> from the north the other has the shelter. It is twisted over with the way
> they be rooting under it for shelter. I don't believe it, but there is
> many a one who would not pass by it at night." Indeed there are

times when the worlds are so near together that it seems as if our earthly chattels were no more than shadows of the things beyond. A lady I knew once saw a village child running about with a long trailing petticoat upon her, and asked the creature why she did not have it cut short. "It was my grandmother's," said the child; "would you have her going about yonder with her petticoat up to her knees, and she dead but four days?" I have read a story of a woman whose ghost haunted her people because they had made her grave-clothes so short that the fires of purgatory burned her knees. The peasantry expect to have beyond the grave houses much like their earthly homes, only there the thatch will never grow leaky, nor the white walls lose their lustre, nor shall the dairy be at any time empty of good milk and butter. But now and then a landlord or an agent or a gauger will go by begging his bread, to show how God divides the righteous from the unrighteous.

Notice in the last sentences that Yeats brings up the idea that the perfect life after death will be a recreation of the present world without any of the burdens of present reality — the cottage will never be leaky, never need painting or whitewashing, and will always be filled with milk and butter (certainly not margarine for the Irish). For us today I suppose such an afterworld would offer a house warm all winter without an oil or a gas bill.

For Yeats this kind of dreaming of the perfect place of heaven was really a continuation of the Celtic imagination. In looking at Irish history we have seen reasons for the survival of a folk culture that sustains such a folk imagination. I also suspect something that Yeats didn't mention: while the peasantry have a sense of heaven, as Yeats would call it, from their Celtic imagination, they also need to generate an optimistic outlook in an attempt to overcome their dismal and impoverished reality. On my first trip to Ireland, many years ago, I was introduced into a cottage in Mayo, a tiny little cottage. It contained only three chairs, just enough for the husband, wife, and child who lived in the cottage. It happened to be a Sunday afternoon, and Sunday dinner was going on, a chicken having been killed to be eaten that day. Someone had laid newspapers on the table to serve as a tablecloth. The husband invited me to share the chicken. He then turned and introduced me to the odd-looking woman who stood by the turf fire in the fireplace stirring a large kettle. She raised her head and asked, in a somewhat strange way, where I was from. I said I came from the United States. Her

16. The natural beauty of an Irish landscape, here in County Kerry.

response was one I have never forgotten. In a soft and sad cadence she sighed "If I had a wish to be born again, I'd wish to be born in a country other than this one of poverty and desolation." It's a line right out of an Irish play.

Notice the outlook: she yearns for a country other than the one that she's in, she wishes to be born in a country other than one of poverty and desolation. She dreams of a perfect place without the burdens of present reality because she wants to escape those burdens. Yeats' early verse dreams of this kind of place, a realm that he called, quite directly, "The Land of The Heart's Desire." He uses this title for a one-act play about the longing for a world which recreates the human world without the effort and the pains of humanity in it.

The poems express a similar wish to transform the Irish country scene to a heavenly realm. We can see this in "The Stolen Child." The poem mentions specific places around Sligo: Sleuth Wood, Rosses, and the Glencar waterfall. The poem is built on the folk belief that Irish fairies can appear and steal a child away and bring him from the human world to the land of the fairy, a marvelous place where one can dance away all night and never feel tired (and probably drink a little bit and never have a hangover). But whatever its full extent, it's a place without trouble.

The poem is spoken by one of the fairies who is trying to lure a child away from the human world. By the last stanza the child does go off with the fairy, but then, interestingly enough, Yeats laments rather than celebrates that decision.

The poem reads:

Where dips the rocky highland
Of Sleuth Wood in the lake,
There lies a leafy island
Where flapping herons wake
The drowsy water-rats;
There we've hid our faery vats,
Full of berries
And of reddest stolen cherries.
Come away, O human child!
To the waters and the wild
With a faery, hand in hand,
For the world's more full of weeping than you can understand.

Where the wave of moonlight glosses
The dim grey sands with light,
Far off by furthest Rosses
We foot it all the night,
Weaving olden dances,
Mingling hands and mingling glances
Till the moon has taken flight;
To and fro we leap
And chase the frothy bubbles,
While the world is full of troubles
And is anxious in its sleep.
Come away, O human child!
To the waters and the wild
With a faery, hand in hand,
For the world's more full of weeping than you can understand.

Where the wandering water gushes
From the hills above Glen-Car,
In pools among the rushes
That scarce could bathe a star,
We seek for slumbering trout
And whispering in their ears
Give them unquiet dreams;
Leaning softly out
From ferns that drop their tears
Over the young streams.
Come away, O human child!
To the waters and the wild
With a faery, hand in hand,
For the world's more full of weeping than you can understand.

Away with us he's going,
The solemn-eyed:
He'll hear no more the lowing
Of the calves on the warm hillside
Or the kettle on the hob
Sing peace into his breast,
Or see the brown mice bob
Round and round the oatmeal-chest.
For he comes, the human child,
To the waters and the wild
With a faery, hand in hand,
From a world more full of weeping than he can understand.

So while Yeats expresses this yearning for a marvelous land of the heart's desire, he also has a more realistic side, because when the child does go to the land of the fairy, he'll no longer experience some of the joys of human life. He will escape human sorrow, but he'll no longer, as the poem says, hear the calves lowing on the warm hillside or the kettle whistle softly on the fire. Yeats has a dilemma: he yearns for a heaven, but if he got it he'd miss the earth. His perceptions of an idealized bliss compete with human life, even with its sorrows. Each realm, the heavenly realm and the human realm, has its advantages and its disadvantages. Yeats wants the best of both, the best of the real and the best of the ideal.

Two other early poems are representative. "The Song of the Wandering Aengus" is built on a folk belief that Celtic goddesses can take the form of fish, and in that form enchant men. Aengus, the Celtic god of love, has kisses that turn to birds, so he is usually depicted with birds flying around his head. When Yeats wrote this poem, he was intensely in love with Maude Gonne, the woman who played the role of Cathleen ni Houlihan in the first production of the play. Undoubtedly he had her in mind in the poem, but the poem is not limited by that.

I went out to the hazel wood,
Because a fire was in my head,
And cut and peeled a hazel wand,
And hooked a berry to a thread;
And when white moths were on the wing,
And moth-like stars were flickering out,
I dropped a berry in a stream
And caught a little silver trout.

When I had laid it on the floor
I went to blow the fire aflame,
But something rustled on the floor,
And some one called me by my name:
It had become a glimmering girl
With apple blossom in her hair
Who called me by my name and ran
And faded through the brightening air.

Though I am old with wandering
Through hollow lands and hilly lands,

I will find out where she has gone,
And kiss her lips and take her hands;
And walk among long dappled grass,
And pluck till time and times are done
The silver apples of the moon,
The golden apples of the sun.

Along with the soft and melodic sound in that poem, notice the attention given to color and light. The time is early evening, when the moth-like stars are flickering out. There is a soft half-light, and also an iridescence in the light and in the color. The trout is *silver*, the girl is *glimmering* and fades in the *brightening* air; the speaker will pluck till time and times are done the *silver* apples of the moon, the *golden* apples of the sun. This concern for shimmering light characterizes the early poems of Yeats. With it he lifts the scenes and the places from the Sligo countryside into a dreamy, shifting, ethereal atmosphere. It's near to earth but also near to heaven.

In "He Wishes For The Cloths of Heaven" this concern for color and light is even more emphatic. Yeats likens the sky to embroidered cloth, an iridescent cloth shot through with threads of silver and threads of gold. The actual evening sky becomes the thing that represents his own individual dreams, again an idealized perception.

Had I the heavens' embroidered cloths,
Enwrought with golden and silver light,
The blue and the dim and the dark cloths
Of night and light and the half-light,
I would spread the cloths under your feet:
But I, being poor, have only my dreams;
I have spread my dreams under your feet;
Tread softly because you tread on my dreams.

Having seen how lyrical and melodic Yeats' early poetry is, it's interesting to turn directly to music itself, to some music written about the same period as Yeats' early poems and in a similarly impressionistic vein. The music was composed in response to the Irish countryside, specifically to the seacoast in the west of Ireland, along the Atlantic Ocean, by Arnold Bax, a not particularly well-known composer who was attracted to Celtic material. One of his musical pieces is a tone poem entitled "Cathleen ni Houlihan."

A particularly relevant selection of his is entitled "The Garden of Fand." Fand, another Celtic goddess, is also an enchantress like the glimmering girl in "The Song of the Wandering Aengus." The music imagines the creation of a marvelous island (another land of the heart's desire) that suddenly springs up in the middle of the sea off the Irish coast. The sea is Fand's garden. Bax wrote the following about the composition of his work:

> I suppose one of my most characteristic musical pieces is an orchestral work called "The Garden of Fand" which is entirely enveloped in an atmosphere of the calm Atlantic off the western shores of Ireland and the enchanted islands of which some of the country people still dream.

Bax recognized that the country people of Ireland were lifting the landscape out of reality into a romantic idealization. In front of the musical score Bax outlines his work. His explanatory notes read in part:

> The Garden of Fand is the Sea. . . . In the earlier portion of the work the composer seeks the atmosphere of an enchanted Atlantic. . . . Upon its surface floats a small ship. . . . The little craft is borne on beneath a sky of pearl and amethyst until on the crest of an immense slowly surging wave it is tossed onto the shore of Fand's miraculous island. Here is unhuman revelry, and the voyagers are caught away, unresisting, into the maze of the dance. A pause comes, and Fand sings her song of immortal love . . . the dancing and the feasting begin again, and, finally, the sea rising suddenly overwhelms the whole island. . . . Twilight falls, the sea subsides, and Fand's magical garden island fades out of sight.

Here in a musical presentation is the same kind of concern for light and color that pervades the poetry of the country. The pearl and amethyst sky recalls Yeats' "He Wishes for the Cloths of Heaven." At the end the musical piece returns from the marvelous island to the reality of life as a wave overwhelms the island, and the music returns to a peaceful description of the Irish seacoast.

Thus the countryside of Ireland engenders its imaginative dreams in the minds of the country people. In Yeats' poems the dreams emerge from and are depicted in an idealized landscape of earth and sky. For Bax the dream world emerges from the sea, as an enchanted island.

CHAPTER EIGHT

Realities, Synge, and the West

THE REALITIES OF county life as they are depicted by the playwright John Millington Synge are vastly different from the imagined realm of Bax and Yeats. A great dramatist of Ireland, in my view Ireland's greatest, Synge was born in 1871, like Yeats of Anglo-Irish parentage. He was educated in that Anglo-Irish stronghold, Trinity College, Dublin, and after his time at the university traveled, like many Irish writers — Richard Brinsley Sheridan, Oscar Wilde, George Moore, and George Bernard Shaw — elsewhere. When he left Ireland, he was primarily interested in music. He traveled in Europe, primarily in Germany, and he went to Paris, which in the 1890s was a thriving center of literary and artistic activity.

In Paris Yeats suggested that Synge return to Ireland, to the Aran Islands, to try to capture in his writings the unique and individual life there. A small, grey, rocky cluster off the coast of Galway, the Aran Islands have a hard climate caused by winds that drive in from the Atlantic bringing heavy rain. Life there is meager, hard, and wild. Robert Flaherty captured the sense of life there in his masterful documentary film "Man of Aran." On Yeats' advice, Synge took up residence on the Aran Islands and discovered, indeed was captured by, the realities of Irish peasant life there. An introverted and solitary man, Synge had wandered many of Ireland's country roads. He became a sort of tramp in the Irish countryside, a loner, a solitary type. He was, as a character in one of his plays says:

17. John Synge as drawn by John Butler Yeats, the father of the poet. (Irish Tourist Board)

lonesome all times, and born lonesome, I'm thinking, as the moon
of dawn. . . . It's a lonesome thing to be passing small towns
with the lights shining sideways when the night is down, or going
in strange places with a dog noising before you and a dog noising
behind, or drawn to the cities where you'd hear a voice kissing
and talking deep love in every shadow of the ditch, and you passing
on with an empty, hungry stomach, failing from your heart.

Synge's experience living the stark life of the Aran Islanders
made him admire the strength and tenacity of the peasants; he was
astonished by the basic, hard quality of their life.

Although Synge had a traditional Ascendancy-class
background and education, and had made a typical move to the artistic and cultivated circles of Europe, Synge did participate in Aran
Island life. Of course he, himself, was not a peasant; he was not
from the Irish countryside. But he was something more than a mere
observer. He was able to see, however, things of which the peasants
themselves were not aware because they were too close to them.
While an outsider and an objective observer, Synge was by intuition
and by adoption a participant in peasant life, and he stood in admiration of the peasantry whom he thought the most natural and
unspoiled human beings. Completely lacking artificiality, the
peasants embodied for Synge a wildly natural ideal, wild with a
strength and beauty that he compared with the strength and beauty
of wild horses. In his prose writing about the Aran Islands Synge
pointed out that the peasants had been untouched by much of the
culture and civilization of Europe after the Dark Ages; they had remained isolated, on the fringes of Europe.

The absence of the heavy boot of Europe has preserved to these people
the agile walk of the wild animal, while the general simplicity of their
lives has given them many other points of physical perfection.
Their way of life has never been acted upon by anything much
more artificial than the nests and the burrows of the creatures
that live round them, and they seem, in a certain sense, to approach
more nearly to the finer types of our aristocracies—who are bred
artificially to a natural ideal—than to the labourer or citizen,
as the wild horse resembles the thoroughbred rather than the
hack or the carthorse. Tribes of the same natural development are,
perhaps, frequent in the half-civilised countries, but here a touch
of the refinement of old societies is blended, with singular effect,
among qualities of wild animal.

18. An Aran Island cliffside shore, with the turbulent sea in the foreground and the land at the top of the picture. (Irish Tourist Board)

Notice the high points here, some of them recalling ideas that emerged in our earlier observations on history and literature. First, Europe has not affected the Aran Islanders, the civilizations of Europe being what Synge calls the heavy boot of Europe. It has not touched the peasantry, who show a certain fineness because their natural qualities are blended with qualities which existed in the ancient Celtic societies. And they are natural in their beauty, true thoroughbreds, except that they are *natural* thoroughbreds rather than artificially bred thoroughbreds. He continues:

> These strange men with receding foreheads, high cheekbones, and ungovernable eyes seem to represent some old type found on these few acres at the extreme border of Europe, where it is only in wild jests and laughter that they can express their loneliness and their desolation.

Loneliness and desolation. It is the loneliness and the desolation of the peasants, and their endurance, that Synge highlights in his literary works, especially in his short, but magnificent one-act play, "Riders to the Sea." In this very simple play not much actually occurs on the stage. But there is very important internal or spiritual action, things going on inside of the characters themselves.

The play opens in a small cottage kitchen in the Aran Islands. The audience quickly learns how fragile the cottage is compared to the vastness and fierceness of the weather outside. A storm is brewing; it is a wild night:

> . . . [the] wind is raising the sea, and there was a star up against the moon, and it rising in the night. . . . There's a great roaring in the west, and it's worse it'll be getting when the tides turn to the wind.

In the cottage kitchen are an old mother, her two daughters, and one of her sons. The play focuses on the mother, Maurya. Maurya's husband and four other sons have, at various times in the past, drowned or been lost at sea. Maurya's fifth son, Michael, has been missing at sea for nine days, apparently drowned, but his body has not yet been recovered from the tumultuous sea. The family is sitting, waiting for the fateful news that the body has been recovered. They know it will be bloated, as a body must be that's been floating in the ocean for nine days. The play never moves away from such realities how cruel death by drowning is and what a body would be like after floating in the sea for more than a week. Maurya's sixth and last son, Bartley, is about to take some horses to the Galway Fair, which means he has to go by sea. The mother pleads with him not to go — primarily because of her serious forebodings since her last son went to sea on a stormy night. The answer she gets is, "It's the life of a young man to be going on the sea."

In this barren land, of course, the sea provides most necessities. Little sustenance can be scratched from the rocks of the Aran Islands. Life comes from fishing. Even light comes from the oil from sharks. It is indeed a life closely intertwined with the sea, and Bartley has to go. As he leaves, Maurya laments in a particularly Irish kind of way.

> He's gone now, God spare us, and we'll not see him again. He's gone now, and when the black night is falling I'll have no son left me in the world. . . . In the big world the old people do be leaving things after them for their sons and children, but in this place it's the young men do be leaving things behind for them that do be old.

When Bartley leaves, Maurya is so distressed that she follows after him to give him a bit of a loaf of bread wrapped up in a piece of cloth. Just as soon as she is out of the house her two daughters pull out a bundle of clothes that has recently been delivered to the cottage, clothes taken from a drowned man discovered when the oar of a boat bumped into the corpse. The body was found off the coast of Donegal, quite a distance to the north of the Aran Islands, and there's a question as to whether the corpse could be that of Maurya's son Michael.

The sisters examine the clothes, and one of the girls recognizes the knitting on a stocking because she remembers dropping some stitches. They realize that Michael's corpse has been found, and both immediately break into bitter crying, one of them saying:

> Ah, . . . isn't it a bitter thing to think of him floating that way to the far north, and no one to keen him but the black hags that do be flying on the sea?

And the other sister, lamenting:

> And isn't it a pitiful thing when there's nothing left of a man who
> was a great rower and a fisher, but a bit of an old shirt and a plain
> stocking.

Maurya then returns to the kitchen in great depression, because
she's had a peculiar folk vision. Many people believe that the Irish
have a kind of extra-sensory perception, or that they communicate
things in ways that are beyond most people's comprehension. Once I
was at dinner at a woman't house, who was herself Irish, and as she
sat at the table, she said, "I think there's something terribly wrong
with my brother. I haven't heard from him, and all day long I've
been thinking about him. I think there's a problem." Later during
dinner the telephone rang, and it turned out that her brother had
died rather suddenly that very day. It was a fact. I heard the woman
herself say those statements. How did she know? The brother was
hundreds of miles away, but she was right.

In any case Maurya, in "Riders To The Sea," claims to have
had a vision of her son, Bartley, the son who has just left. She has
seen him riding on a red mare, with a grey pony behind it; riding on
the grey pony is her son Michael, whom the audience knows is dead.
Seeing the two of them that way, Maurya believes that they are now
both dead. Because of this she's in a state of depression when she
returns to the cottage kitchen and sits down to tell her daughters of
her vision. To console her they say nothing like that could happen
because the priest claimed that God wouldn't leave her without a
son. And Maurya answers in this way:

> It's little the like of him knows of the sea. . . . Bartley will be lost
> now, and let you call in Eamon and make me a good coffin out of
> white boards, for I won't live after them. I've had a husband, and
> a husband's father and six sons in this house — six fine men, though
> it was a hard birth I had with every one of them and they coming
> to the world — and some of them were found and some of them
> were not found, but they're gone now the lot of them. . . . There
> were Stephen, and Shawn, were lost in the great wind and found
> after in the Bay of Gregory of the Golden Mouth, and carried up
> the two of them on the one plank, and in by that door. . . . There
> was Sheamus and his father, and his own father again, were lost in
> the dark night, and not a stick or a sign was seen of them when the

19. A curagh, the light boat with a tarred hull of skins or cloth, as used in the Aran Islands. (Irish Tourist Board)

20. An Irish cottage near the sea.

sun went up. There was Patch after was drowned out of a curagh that turned over. I was sitting here with Bartley, and he a baby, lying on my two knees, and I seen two women, and three women, and four women coming in, and they crossing themselves, and not saying a word. I looked out then, and there were men coming after them, and they holding a thing in the half of a red sail, and water dripping out of it—it was a dry day, Nora—and leaving a track to the door.

A few minutes after this Nora looks out and sees some people, as she says, carrying a thing among them, and there's water dripping out of it, leaving a track by the big stones. The corpse of Maurya's last son, Bartley, now drowned, is brought in. Maurya's response to this final death, of her last son, the son she pleaded with not to go to the sea, is really the major focus of the play. This is the internal or, if you wish, spiritual action of the play. Before she struggled fiercely to save Bartley from the sea, but now the intensity of her grief and the intensity of her suffering and desolation have brought her to a calm, a tragic calm. Her last son's death brings her now heightened understanding of the basic and universal condition of all humanity: the tragic condition of mankind.

Maurya's lines in the last part of the play are extraordinary:

> They're all gone now, and there isn't anything more the sea can do to me. . . . I'll have no call now to be up crying and praying when the wind breaks from the south, and you can hear the surf is in the east, and the surf is in the west, making a great stir with the two noises, and they hitting one on the other. I'll have no call now to be going down and getting Holy Water in the dark nights after Samhain [the celebration near the beginning of November], and I won't care what way the sea is when the other women will be keening. Give me the Holy Water, Nora, there's a small sup still on the dresser.

She gets some holy water and drops Michael's clothes across Bartley's feet and sprinkles holy water on the body, saying:

> It isn't that I haven't prayed for you, Bartley, to the almighty God. It isn't that I haven't said prayers in the dark night till you wouldn't know what I'd be saying; but it's a great rest I'll have now, and it's time surely. It's a great rest I'll have now, and great sleeping in the long nights after Samhain, if it's only a bit of wet flour we do have to eat, and maybe a fish that would be stinking.

She kneels down again and crosses herself and says prayers under her breath. Then she stands up slowly, spreads out some pieces of Michael's clothes beside Bartley's body, sprinkling them again with some holy water, and speaks again, putting an empty cup down on the table. Laying her hands together on Bartley's feet, she says:

> They're all together this time, and the end is come. May the Almighty God have mercy on Bartley's soul, and on Michael's soul, and on the souls of Sheamus and Patch, and Stephen and Shawn, and may He have mercy on my soul, Nora, and on the soul of everyone is left living in the world. Michael has a clean burial in the far north, by the grace of the Almighty God. Bartley will have a fine coffin out of white boards, and a deep grave surely. What more can we want than that? No man at all can be living for ever, and we must be satisfied.

The last line of the play is one of the great lines of world drama: "No man at all can be living for ever, and we must be satisfied." In it we see Synge's admiration for the strength of the Irish peasant. Maurya has been through ruthlessly hard realities not only of Irish life but of all life. And in passing through this daunting test, she illustrates the survival of the human spirit. She has complete and utter knowledge of the fierce and unrelenting force of the sea, of nature. But in her the human spirit survives. She knows the full realities, and her endurance and her suffering bring her not only to an understanding, but to an acceptance and affirmation of life and man's position in an overwhelmingly powerful universe. She has, in a sense, said *Yes* to life even at this most heart breaking moment.

Yeats said that the intensity of the grief at the end of this play was:

> . . . carried beyond grief into pure contemplation. . . . The persons upon the stage . . . greaten till they are *humanity itself*. We feel our minds . . . spread out slowly . . . carried beyond time and persons to where passion, living through its thousand purgatorial years . . . becomes wisdom.

Another difficult reality no Irish country people could overlook was emigration—people, family, leaving Ireland. This fact touches many Americans, whose forebears, years ago, wrenched themselves from family and home and made the very difficult journey across the Atlantic to struggle through hard work, often in very alien circumstances, in the United States. When these emigrants left, they left permanently; they never saw their families again. Things have changed considerably now, of course, with air travel. Separations from families in Ireland are now not the same as they were.

From the years of the famine, in the 1840s, until very recently, Ireland's annual emigration rate exceeded its birth rate. That means, of course, that more people were leaving Ireland than were born there. Liam O'Flaherty's short story "Going Into Exile" captures the cruel facts and emotions that occurred for decades in innumerable country places across Ireland when children went out to the United States, to England, to Australia, or to other places.

The story begins at a party in a country cottage, Patrick Feeney's cottage. The party is a farewell for his eldest son and daughter, Michael and Mary, who are going to the United States the next day. Patrick Feeney and his wife will probably never see them again. The Irish call such parties American wakes. O'Flaherty describes carefully and accurately the details of the cottage, the family preparation throughout the party, the clothes worn, the dancing, the music, the festivities. Against this background there are moments which suggest the unspoken turmoil going on inside the parents and inside the children.

> Towards dawn, when the floor was crowded with couples, arranged in fours, stamping on the floor and going to and fro, dancing the "Walls of Limerick," Feeney was going out to the gable when his son Michael followed him out. The two of them walked side by side about the yard over the grey sea pebbles that had been strewn there the previous day. They walked in silence and yawned without need, pretending to be taking the air. But each of them was very excited; Michael was taller than his father and not so thickly built, but the shabby blue serge suit that he had bought for going to America was too narrow for his broad shoulders and the coat was too wide around the waist. He moved clumsily in it and his hands appeared altogether too bony and big and red, and he didn't know what to do with them. During his twenty-one years of life he had never worn anything other than the homespun clothes of Inverara, and the shop-made clothes appeared as strange to him and as uncomfortable as a dress suit worn by a man working in a sewer. His face was flushed a bright red and his blue eyes shone with excitement. Now and again he wiped the perspiration from his forehead with the lining of his gray tweed cap.
>
> At last Patrick Feeney reached his usual position at the gable end. He halted, balanced himself on his heels with his hands in his waist belt, coughed and said: "It's going to be a warm day". The son came up beside him, folded his arms, and leaned his right shoulder against the gable.
>
> "It was kind of Uncle Ned to lend the money for the dance, father," he said. "I'd hate to think that we'd have to go without something or other, just the same as everybody else. I'll send you that money, the very first money I earn, father . . . even before I pay Aunt Mary for my passage money. I should have all that money paid off in four months, and then I'll have some more money to send you by Christmas."
>
> And Michael felt very strong and manly recounting what he was going to do when he got to Boston, Massachusetts. He told himself that with his great strength he would earn a great deal of money. Conscious of his youth and his strength and lusting for an adven-

turous life, for the moment he forgot the ache in his heart that the thought of leaving his father inspired in him.

The father was silent for some time. He was looking at the sky, with his lower lip hanging, thinking of nothing. At last he sighed as a memory struck him. "What is it?" said the son. "Don't weaken for God's sake. You'll only make it hard for me." "Fooh!" said the father suddenly with pretended gruffness. "Who is weakening? I'm afraid your new clothes make you impudent." Then he was silent for a moment and continued in a low voice: "I was thinking of that potato field you sowed alone last spring the time I had influenza. I never set eyes on a man that could do it better. It's a cruel world that takes you away from the land that God made you for."

"Oh, what are you talking about, father?" asid Michael irritably. "Sure what did anybody get out of the land but poverty and hard work and potatoes and salt?"

"Ah, yes," said the father with a sigh, "but it's your own, the land, and over there"—he waved his hand at the western sky—"you'll be giving your sweat to some other man's land, or what's equal to it."

"Indeed," muttered Michael, looking at the ground with a melancholy expression in his eyes," it's poor encouragement you are giving me."

They stood in silence for fully five minutes. Each hungered to embrace the other, to cry, to beat the air, to scream with excess of sorrow. But they stood silent and sombre, like nature about them, hugging their woe. Then they went back to the cabin.

There are similar scenes throughout the story. As daylight comes, we get another careful description, this time of the daughter Mary, who is also "going out." She wears a navy blue skirt and white blouse and is crushing a handkerchief between her palms with a combination of feverish excitement, fear, and loathing of leaving home. Mrs. Feeney keeps her busy with the party, but Mrs. Feeney herself is troubled by her emotions.

"Oh, well, God is good" said Mrs. Feeney, as she wiped her lips with the tip of her bright, clean, check apron. "What will be must be, and sure there is hope from the sea, but there is no hope from the grave. It's sad and poor to have to suffer but. . . ." Mrs. Feeney stopped suddenly, aware that all these platitudes meant nothing whatsoever. Like her husband she was unable to think intelligently about her two children going away. Whenever the reality of their going away, maybe forever, three thousand miles into a vast unknown world, came before her mind, it seemed that a thin bar of some hard metal thrust itself forward from her brain and rested behind the wall of her forehead. So that almost immediately she became stupidly conscious of the pain caused by the imaginary bar of metal and she forgot the dread prospect of her children going away. But her mind grappled with the things about her busily and efficiently, with the preparation of food, with the entertainment of her guests, with the numerous little things that have to be done in a house when there is a party and which only a woman can do properly. These little things, in a manner, saved her, for the moment at least, from bursting into tears whenever she looked at her daughter and whenever she thought of her son, whom she loved most of all her children, because perhaps she nearly died giving birth to him and he had been very delicate until he was twelve years old. So she laughed down in her breast a funny little laugh that she had made that made her heave where her check apron rose out from the waistband and in a deep curve. "A person begins to talk," she said with a shrug of her shoulders sideways, "and then a person says foolish things."

"That's true," said the old peasant, noisily pouring more tea from his cup to his saucer.

As daylight comes, the party ends. The family sits awkwardly to have breakfast, and then they clean up. The time for the parting has come. The last part of O'Flaherty's story presents the feelings of the final moment, feelings that must have been common for all who lived through such moments.

At last everything was ready. Mrs. Feeney had exhausted all excuses for moving about, engaged on trivial tasks. She had to go into the big bedroom where Mary was putting on her new hat. The mother sat on a chair by the window, her face contorting on account of the flood of tears she was keeping back. Michael moved about the room uneasily, his two hands knotting a big red handkerchief behind his back. Mary twisted about in front of the mirror that hung over the black wooden mantlepiece. She was spending a long time with the hat. It was the first one she had ever worn, but it fitted her beautifully, and it was in excellent taste. It was given to her by the schoolmistress, who was very fond of her, and she herself had taken it in a little. She had an instinct for beauty in dress and deportment.

But the mother, looking at how well her daughter wore the cheap navy blue costume and the white frilled blouse, and the little round black hat with the fat, fluffy, glossy curl covering each ear, and the black silk stockings with the blue clocks in them, and the little black shoes that had laces of three colors in them, got suddenly enraged with. . . . She didn't know with what she got enraged. But for the moment she hated her daughter's beauty, and she remembered all the anguish of giving birth to her, and nursing her and toiling for her, for no other purpose than to lose her now and let her go away, maybe to be ravished wantonly because of her beauty and her love of gaiety. A cloud of mad jealousy and mad hatred against this impersonal beauty that she saw in her daughter almost suffocated the mother, and she stretched out her hands in front of her unconsciously and then just as suddenly her anger vanished like a puff of smoke, and she burst into wild tears, wailing: "My children, oh, my children, far over the sea you'll be carried from me, your mother." And she began to rock herself and she threw her apron over her head.

Immediately the cabin was full of the sound of bitter wailing. A dismal cry rose from the women gathered in the kitchen. "Far over the sea they will be carried," began woman after woman, and they all rocked themselves and hid their heads in their aprons. Michael's mongrel dog began to howl on the hearth. Little Thomas sat down on the hearth beside the dog and, putting his arms around him, he began to cry, although he didn't know exactly why he was crying, but he felt melancoly on account of the dog howling and so many people being about.

In the bedroom the son and daughter, on their knees, clung to their mother, who held their heads between her hands and rained kisses on both heads ravenously. After the first wave of tears she had stopped weeping. The tears still ran down her cheeks, but her eyes gleamed and they were dry. There was a fierce look in them as she searched all over the heads of her two children with them, with her brows contracted, searching with a fierce terror-stricken expression, as if by the intensity of her stare she hoped to keep a living photograph of them before her mind. With her quivering lips she made a queer sound, like "im-m-m-m" and she kept kissing. Her right hand clutched at Mary's left shoulder and with her left she fondled the back of Michael's neck. The two children were sobbing freely. They must have stayed that way a quarter of an hour.

Then the father came into the room, dressed in his best clothes. He wore a new frieze waistcoat, with a gray and black front and a white back. He held his soft black felt hat in one hand and in the other he had a bottle of holy water. He coughed and said in a weak gentle voice that was strange to him as he touched his son: "Come now, it is time."

Michael and Mary got to their feet. The father sprinkled them with holy water and they crossed themselves. Then without looking at their mother, who lay in the chair with her hands clasped on her lap, looking at the ground in a silent tearless stupor, they left the room. Each hurriedly kissed little Thomas, who was not going to Kilmurrage, and then, hand in hand, they left the house. As Michael was going out the door he picked a piece of loose whitewash from the wall and put it in his pocket. The people filed out after them, down the yard and on the road, like a funeral procession. The mother was left in the house with little Thomas and two old peasant women from the village. Nobody spoke in the cabin for a long time.

Then the mother rose and came into the kitchen. She looked at the two women, and her little son and at the hearth, as if she were looking for something she had lost. Then she threw her hands into the air and ran out into the yard.

"Come back," she screamed, "Come back to me."

She looked wildly down the road with dilated nostrils, her bosom heaving. But there was nobody in sight. Nobody replied. There was a crooked stretch of limestone road, surrounded by gray crags that were scorched by the sun. The road ended in a hill and then dropped out of sight. The hot June day was silent. Listening foolishly for an answering cry, the mother imagined she could hear the crags simmering under the hot rays of the sun. It was something in her head that was singing.

The two old women led her back into the kitchen. "There is nothing that time will not cure," said one. "Yes. Time and patience," said the other.

And thus the story ends. The story is a fine achievement and very central and faithful to the Irish experience. O'Flaherty doesn't step out of the range of the people in the story; very carefully, throughout the story, he gives a compelling sense of repressed emotion, of emotion kept in check until the end of the story.

Another work which presents explicitly and with feeling the facts and interior emotions of emigration is a wonderful play by the contemporary Irish writer Brian Friel entitled "Philadelphia Here I Come."

In considering how life in the Irish countryside has been portrayed, we started out with Yeats' idyllic and lushly beautiful poetic evocation of the scenery and the peasant life in Ireland. We then looked at the loneliness and desolation of Synge's Aran Islanders and at the sadness felt when family members emigrated. But along with the sadness, the strength, and the tenacity of the Irish peasantry in Synge and O'Flaherty, we must add another dimension to the character of life in the Irish countryside. We noticed that Synge admired the unspoiled strength, wild beauty, or natural nobility of the isolated Irish country people. One comparison he made was of the peasants to wild horses.

It's good to keep this admiration in mind as we approach "The Playboy of the Western World," a comic play of Synge's, quite different from "Riders To The Sea." It was first produced in the Abbey Theatre in 1907, two years before Synge died at age thirty-seven. The play is rich in its reflections and revelations about life of the Irish countryside.

Since the play has a complicated story, with many twists and turns, a complete telling of the plot would not be especially helpful. Instead, I'll extract certain significant elements which reflect on life in general in the countryside.

As Synge himself said, there are several sides to the play. A primary thread in the plot deals with the relationship of a country boy with his father.

The play opens in a country pub "on the wild coast of County Mayo." In the pub sits a girl, Pegeen, often called Pegeen Mike because her father's name is Mike and that's how country Irish clarify identity. Pegeen is the pub owner's daughter and she is, at the moment, in charge of the pub. As she sits there, a stranger arrives, a very slight, tired, dirty, and somewhat frightened young man, named Christy Mahon. The country people in the pub stare at him. In conversation Christy hints that he's been on the road for some days, hiding in ditches and in the bushes because maybe the police are looking for him. Eventually, through skillful Irish conversational probing, the others in the pub get some information from him.

I learned myself in Ireland that the Irish rarely ask people they meet for the first time many direct "personal" questions. In America people say, "Who are you? Where are you from? Where did you go to school? What to you do for a living?" and so on. In Ireland people consider such behavior somewhat impertinent. If a stranger wants to reveal information, he can do so and they'll be delighted to have it. Of course, the Irish may say certain kinds of things to *elicit* that information, but they won't ask direct questions. If you ask direct questions, no information whatsoever is forthcoming. But if you hold your peace for a while, eventually you learn what you want to know.

The people in the pub converse so skillfully that they eventually learn Christy has killed his father, his Da. This scared and quivering little man acknowledges that in a sudden, unpremeditated, almost reflex, action against the tyranny of his father, who has apparently ordered him about for years, he has committed not merely murder, but patricide.

Christy had been digging potatoes under his father's superior and irritating command. One more order came, the last straw for Christy, so he picked up the shovel and bashed it down on his father's head. Such a sudden burst of anger, a kind of anger nobody thought meek Christy capable of, even came as a surprise to Christy, who tells the people in the pub this information rather reluctantly. He certainly is not proud of his action and he's scared. It's only because Pegeen taunts him as he is speaking mysteriously about some bad deed he has done that he says what he's done. Pegeen says, to irritate him, "You did nothing at all. A soft lad the like of you wouldn't slit the windpipe of a screeching sow." Christy, offended, answers, "You're not speaking the truth." And Pegeen, miffed at being called a liar, says, "Not speaking the truth, is it? Would you have me knock the head of you with the butt of the broom?" At which Christy sharply cries out, "Don't strike me. I killed my poor father Tuesday was a week, for doing the like of that. . . . With the help of God I did surely, and that the Holy Immaculate Mother may intercede for his soul."

This last little invocation hardly calls to mind a heartless murderer. Amazed and fascinated the group in the pub want to hear all the details of the murder. As the play develops, scared little Christy becomes a greatly admired and sought-after hero. The people in the pub apparently think he's wonderful, that he's done a brave and marvelous deed. And he, himself, begins to believe that he's pretty brave and marvelous after a while. It's a whole new experience for him. By the end of Act I, when the curtain is closing and Christy is going to bed in the pub for the night — he's going to stay on for awhile — he says, "It's great luck and company I've won me in the end of time—two fine women fighting for the likes of me—till I'm thinking this night wasn't I a foolish fellow not to kill my father in the years gone by." He's delighted with himself and the marvels his murderous deed has wrought.

By Act II, though, we learn that Christy hadn't really done a complete job on his father. The father, with a bandage on his head, appears in the town, searching for his son. Christy doesn't meet his father until Act III, by which time Christy has developed enough as a hero to be in full command of himself. As a matter of fact he's just won athletic competitions with the local athletes, so he's more of a hero than ever. When everyone in the village learns that Christy hasn't really killed his father as he said, he loses his heroic stature and is disgraced. The people in the town are irritated because they thought they had a bona fide murderer when, it turns out, they just have a liar; they're most disappointed.

Because of their name-calling Christy gets angry enough to chase after his father a second time. He runs out of the pub and, we're led to believe, strikes his father over the head a second time, this time with full effect. He returns to the pub to claim his laurels. But a peculiar thing happens. This time, the "second time" he has killed his father, the deed has occurred on the scene, and the people in the pub, rather than think he's wonderful, turn against Christy as a criminal and start taking justice into their own hands. They tie him up and get him ready to be hanged as punishment for this murder. But again, and not too surprisingly, Christy hasn't done the job completely, and his father manages to stumble into the pub just as the people in the pub are tying Christy up.

The father, in irritation, takes the ropes off of Christy, and with great respect for one another and as great friends, the father and son go walking off together. Christy has won his father's admiration because the father now sees that Christy is a man . . . he can stand up and defend himself. Christy announces to his father that he, Christy, is going to be the master of all fights from now on, and the father is proud of Christy's new ability. The two of them go out blessing the people in the pub. Christy says as he exits:

Ten thousand blessings upon all that's here, for you've turned me a likely gaffer in the end of all, the way I'll go romancing through a romping lifetime from this hour to the dawning of the judgment day.

The first thing to notice in this plot thread is the father-son relationship. The father's severity, Christy himself says, results from age — the father is getting old and crusty. The people in the pub immediately understand this severity in the father, and they symnpathize with Christy. Pegeen Mike's irascible father is another presentation of an Irish country father. The domineering father who continues to order his grown up son about is perhaps more familiar to Irishmen, and more immediately understood by Irishmen, than by an audience in the United States.

Extraordinary parental power, often including economic power, characterized Irish country life at the time the play was written. Men frequently married women somewhat younger than themselves, and very often the eldest son brought his wife to live in his parents' cottage. In "Cathleen ni Houlihan" Michael Gillane, if he had lived to marry Delia, would have brought her into the household of his mother and father and the two would have remained under the dominance of his parents. And *young* children were meant to be seen, not heard.

The first time I went to Ireland, to County Mayo, I was, as a visiting school teacher, supposed to have a session of conversation with the local school teacher, Master Kelly. Master Kelly came over to the house of an evening, and three chairs were placed around the turf fire in the fireplace for the three men, Master Kelly, my host, and me. My host's two children, one fourteen and the other seventeen, had to put on their Sunday clothes — suits, ties, white shirts — in honor of the event. When Master Kelly arrived about ten o'clock, they greeted him, and then the men sat down to have a conversation, with the help of some bottles of Guinness. The two sons sat with their backs to the wall from ten until about midnight, listening in silence. They were supposed to be attentive to and perhaps even enlightened by the conversation. About midnight their father turned to them and said, "You may go to bed now." They said goodnight to me and to Mr. Kelly and to their father and went off to bed. Master Kelly stayed on until three o'clock.

I simply can't imagine an American fourteen-year-old getting dressed up to sit, back to the wall, not saying a word, for two hours. It illustrates the kind of dominance that I'm talking about. If that dominance continues as an Irish lad grows older, somehow or other he has to assert himself. In "Playboy of the Western World" it's an extremely violent assertion — he hits his father on the head with the potato shovel. But the father recognizes what the act means—that his son has become a man. The two of them can now go off romping together, as Christy says, to the day of judgment. In so doing he doubtless strikes a chord of sympathy and understanding in an Irish audience.

Another aspect of country life to notice in this plot thread is that it hardly occurs to anybody in the pub to turn Christy over to the police when he first tells them how he killed his father. Rather than turn him over to the police, they're delighted with the information and want to hear all the details of the murder. The second time he commits murder they plan to take care of him themselves. We have here Irish folk justice at work. At the time of the play representatives of the British government, at least as the Irish perceived the situation, administered Ireland's official judicial system. Moreover this system had been laid on top of a traditional Irish system, so it was not much respected. Country people apparently tended to employ their own justice system, for to cooperate with the Crown would be, in a sense, to participate in something that they felt was alien.

In the play the pub itself is described as a shebeen, which is a somewhat illegal pub. It's folly to try unraveling here the complications of Irish drinking laws, but they explicitly set serving hours in the day and so on. At the time of this play most of those laws could be suspended if somebody was a bona fide traveler. Although a pub legally had to close at a certain hour, if a patron qualified as a bona fide traveler—I think the person had to have traveled at least three miles—the pub could serve beyond those hours. So in "Playboy" all the people in the pub laboriously point out the complicated, long road they had to travel to get there. They explain that they have to turn this way and that way to reach the pub. Actually, of course, they are local inhabitants, who can get there in no time at all by leaping over some stones in a brook. Needless to say this is the route they take, but their stories qualify them as bona fide travelers. We have already a rather slippery lack of respect for the law.

Irish folk law continued in the countryside for centuries. It was their law and the people took care of things in their own way, rather than cooperate with an alien system of British justice.

There's a wonderful short story (it's also been made into a short play) by Frank O'Connor entitled "In The Train," about an Irish woman from a small town who poisons her husband because she wants a lover. Because she has committed murder, she is being tried by the Court in Dublin. The townspeople go to Dublin, and one by one they get up and testify that she is a fine woman and that of course she would never kill her husband, and so on. Because of this string of character references, she is acquitted of the murder. Everybody in town gets back on the train to return home. One by one the townspeople sit down next to the woman and tell her that of course they know she killed her husband, and of course they had lied. They promise they'll take care of her in their own way when they get back home and warn her not to feel too comforted about her acquittal. They promise she will be ostracized and forced to live with that knowledge. Only hours before they all swore on the Bible that she was an upright woman. But that's in the Court House. At home they'll apply their own country justice. O'Connor neatly focuses attention on the dual outlook on law in the countryside. This same system of countryside justice is evident in "Playboy."

Many people think that Synge, by having the peasantry idolize Christy when they hear that he's a murderer the first time, and then by having them want to string him up when they actually see him strike his father over the head the second time, was showing that the peasantry couldn't tell the difference between a good story and a real fact. Some say Synge's point was that the peasantry were dumb or even ludicrous in their limited understanding. I've seen a production of the play based in this assumption. The peasants fell over one another like clowns or drunken boobs. I dismiss this interpretation completely; Synge had a strong and permanent admiration for the peasantry. While he observed the life of the country dweller objectively, he would never have suggested that they were lunatic, dumb, or inept in any kind of way.

What aggravates the people in the pub the second time Christy hits his father over the head with the shovel is not that he's a murderer, but that they've been duped. They feel betrayed. Here they thought Christy a daring murderer and he really wasn't. Pegeen herself confesses this directly: "It's lies you told, letting on you had him slitted, and you nothing at all." She is so irritated that she's been fooled, her attraction to him does a turnabout.

Another plot element of interest in terms of country life is marriage. When the play opens, Pegeen is making plans for her marriage to a local boy named Shawn Keogh. After Christy arrives and becomes the idol of the village, many local women, including

Pegeen, start to pursue him. Besides Pegeen, a relatively well-fixed widow, the Widow Quin, has set her sights on Christy. Pegeen finds Christy so enchanting she's ready to give up her financée, and her father, too, approves of Christy as a son-in-law. Each possible marriage reflects a particular attitude towards marriage. First there's the possible alliance between Pegeen and Shawn Keogh. In the isolated countryside of Mayo, there isn't much choice for a girl in a small town, a town Pegeen describes as "a poor thatched place." The play assumes that she must choose from what's available locally. While Pegeen is a woman of spirit and spunk, she has made plans to marry Sean Keogh because he's about all that's available. He may be ordinary, even gutless, but he's her age, he's possible. The marriage is the expected, inevitable one that occurs in a small town — it's a product of the landscape. It's the equivalent in the United States of a high school cheer leader marrying the boy from down the street who plays on the football team. Their parents are good friends, the kids like one another in high school, it seems "right" that they should get married, and indeed they do. They stay in the same town and on life goes. The people involved haven't looked elsewhere, haven't gone elsewhere, haven't waited to see if they change their minds, or develop in a different way. And in Ireland the geographical limitations of choice are further exacerbated by economic limitations.

The second possible marriage, of the Widow Quin to Christy, reveals her attitude that marriage is a serious economic transaction. It's a great way to step up in life and get some security. She points out to Christy that because she's a widow, she has a bit more of this world's goods — land, a house, and some cattle. If Christy marries her, he'll be comfortable and well fixed and she'll take care of him. To marry her would be "a good deal." As long as one's going to get married, she seems to think, why not marry somebody with a little cash? If one has the choice, why not make oneself a little more comfortable?

Then we have the attitude of Pegeen's father. He prefers to have Pegeen marry Christy rather than Shawn Keogh because he regards marriage as primarily for breeding, for getting children. And if he's going to get some grandchildren, he wants good, strong grandchildren from able, sturdy stock, so his girl's got to marry "a tough," and Christy is tougher than Shawn. As he says, marriage is really bulls and heifers, a kind of animal husbandry.

Set against these three attitudes towards marriage—marriage as a geographic inevitability, marriage as a bargain, and marriage as a breeding stall—is the love that develops between Pegeen and Christy, or marriage as a romantic excursion. Their rather innocent, vernal, and idealized love is expressed in romantic, lyrical terminology. It's a fragile bubble that floats rather beautifully over this "poor thatched place," this rugged, alien landscape. In the third act of the play Christy and Pegeen have a short, touching love scene (if it qualifies as a love scene—they don't even hold hands). In films in the United States a similar pair would often have their clothes off in the same amount of time, but in Ireland Christy and Pegeen just talk to each other lyrically. The scene is short enough to be worth quoting. Christy has just won an athletic competition and he's at the height of his self-approval. He's ecstatic. He has developed into a mature human being in several ways during the play, and he now feels confident enough to ask Pegeen to marry him.

He comes in from the competition, looks at Pegeen with delight, and says:

> *Christy:* "I'll have great times if I win the crowning prize I'm seeking now, and that's your promise that you'll wed me in a fortnight, when our banns is called."
>
> *Pegeen:* "You've right daring to go ask me that, when all knows you'll be starting to some girl in your own townland, when your father's rotten in four months, or five."
>
> *Christy:* "Starting from you, is it? I will not, then, and when the airs is warming in four months, or five, it's then yourself and me should be pacing Neifin in the dews of night, the times sweet smells do be rising, and you'd see a little shiny new moon, maybe, sinking on the hills."
>
> *Pegeen:* "And it's that kind of a poacher's love you'd make, Christy Mahon, on the sides of Neifin, when the night is down?"
>
> *Christy:* "It's little you'll think if my love's a poacher's, or an earl's itself, when you'll feel my two hands stretched around you, and I squeezing kisses on your puckered lips, till I'd feel a kind of pity for the Lord God is all ages sitting lonesome in his golden chair."
>
> *Pegeen:* "That'll be right fun, Christy Mahon, and any girl would walk her heart out before she'd meet a young man was your like for eloquence, or talk, at all."
>
> *Christy:* "Let you wait, to hear me talking, till we're astray in Erris, when Good Friday's by, drinking a sup from a well,

and making mighty kisses with our wetted mouths, or gaming in
a gap or sunshine, with yourself stretched back unto your
necklace, in the flowers of the earth."

Pegeen: "I'd be nice so, is it?"

Christy: "If the mitred bishops seen you that time, they'd be the
like of the holy prophets, I'm thinking, do be straining the
bars of paradise to lay eyes on the Lady Helen of Troy,
and she abroad, pacing back and forward, with a nosegay in
her golden shawl."

Pegeen: "And what is it I have, Christy Mahon, to make me
fitting entertainment for the like of you, that has such poet's
talking, and such bravery of heart?"

Christy: "Isn't there the light of seven heavens in your heart
alone, the way you'll be an angel's lamp to me from this out,
and I abroad in the darkness, spearing salmons in the Owen,
or the Carrowmore?"

Pegeen: "If I was your wife, I'd be along with you those nights,
Christy Mahon, the way you'd see I was a great hand at
coaxing bailiffs, or coining funny nick-names for the stars of
night."

Christy: "You, is it? Taking your death in the hailstones, or in
the fogs of dawn."

Pegeen: "Yourself and me would shelter easy in a narrow
bush, but we're only talking, maybe, for this would be a poor,
thatched place to hold a fine lad is the like of you."

Christy: "If I wasn't a good Christian, it's on my naked knees
I'd be saying my prayers and paters to every jackstraw you
have roofing your head, and every stony pebble is paving the
laneway to your door."

Pegeen: "If that's the truth, I'll be burning candles from this
out to the miracles of God that have brought you from the
south to-day, and I, with my gowns bought ready, the way that
I can wed you, and not wait at all."

Christy: "It's miracles, and that's the truth. Me there toiling a long
while, not knowing at all I was drawing all times nearer
to this holy day."

Pegeen: "And myself, a girl, was tempted often to go sailing
the seas till I'd marry a Jew-man, with ten kegs of gold,
and I not knowing at all there was the like of you drawing
nearer, like the stars of God."

Christy: "And to think I'm long years hearing women talking
that talk, to all bloody fools, and this the first time I've
heard the like of your voice talking sweetly for my own
delight."

Pegeen: "And to think it's me is talking sweetly, Christy Mahon, and I the fright of seven townlands for my biting tongue. Well, the heart's a wonder; and, I'm thinking, there won't be our like in Mayo, for gallant lovers, from this hour, to-day."

And then the father enters abruptly, singing drunkenly, and the love scene ends.

For Christy and for Pegeen, this is a very real flight of romantic love, but it cannot, rather sadly, be sustained; it cannot survive in the reality of the poor thatched place. Their attraction is deeply affecting, but this very real moment is also one of great fragility. It's almost as though Synge has carefully placed an escapist flight, a *dream* of love, against the background of marriage as a bargain, as animal husbandry, or as an inevitable union of local folk. Synge objectively sees the local realities, but he also sees and feels the soaring romance, the yearning after love and bliss; the contrast between this yearning and the reality of life in Mayo is one of the play's central tensions. Life seldom, and then only briefly, measures up to the ideal that the heart yearns for. And for Synge, it seems, the joys of first love are never equaled. The Irish countryside, the poor thatched place, works against romantic idealism, but nevertheless romantic idealism is an aspect of reality—it's a part of the larger landscape of life.

Synge's life has a bearing on this aspect of the play. He had fallen in love himself for the first time with a girl named Molly Allgood. Synge was in his mid-thirties, but in Ireland that's not a surprising age for first love. Molly Allgood was an actress, and it was she who played Pegeen in the first production of "Playboy of the Western World" in 1907. Synge, in his shy and introverted way, was courting Molly, but during rehearsal both of them thought that nobody knew about it. Actually everybody in the cast knew. Synge and Molly would pretend mere acquaintance, and then they would leave the rehearsals separately and meet one another around the corner.

The lyric flight in the play gives evidence of what Synge himself was probably feeling for Molly at the time. He and Molly never married. Synge's increasing illness worked against it, as did the reality that Molly was a Roman Catholic and Synge was Protestant gentry. Synge died from his illness in 1909, with Molly, who nursed him in his sickness, in attendance.

21. The remains of a late nineteenth-century house in the country, now with a metal roof and used as a small barn. This house was the birth place of the author's grandfather.

Finally, we should not overlook the short preface to the play Synge wrote, because it directs us to what he thought was important. Speaking of the Irish peasantry Synge says:

> . . . I am glad to acknowledge how much I owe to the folk-imagination of these fine people . . . in countries where the imagination of the people, and the language they use, is rich and living, it is possible for a writer to be rich and copious in his words, and at the same time to give the reality, which is the root of all poetry. . . . On the state one must have reality, and one must have joy; . . . the rich joy found only in what is superb and wild in reality. . . . In Ireland, for a few years more, we have a popular imagination that is fiery and magnificent, and tender; so that those of us who wish to write start with a chance that's not given to writers in places where the springtime of the local life has been forgotten, and the harvest is a memory only, and the straw has been turned into bricks.

For Synge, the Irish countryside and the Irish peasantry had a folk imagination, copious words, a wild reality, and a joy that Synge thought would be lost when modern, more commercial life came along, when, as he says at the end of the preface, "the straw has been turned into bricks." What effect the present economic development in the Irish countryside will have on this folk imagination is a question.

22. The mature Yeats with his children, Michael and Anne. (Irish Tourist Board)

CHAPTER NINE

Mature Destinations

IRELAND'S greatest poet, William Butler Yeats, is one of those artists whose life was long enough and whose development and ideas and techniques were complicated enough so that we can divide his works into periods. His early poems, such as "The Stolen Child," "The Song of the Wandering Aengus," and "He Wishes for the Cloths of Heaven," are dreamy and somewhat ethereal with a yearning for a more perfect world than the world that we live in. Yeats sometimes associated the perfect world with that of Irish myth and Yeats makes the mythological world seem more desirable than the present reality. He created his own "land of the heart's desire," with undulating, melodic lines, lush tones, and iridescent images.

The poetry from Yeats' later period is quite different in tone and technique. Much less dreamy, occasionally somewhat cynical, Yeats seems to face more directly the harder and harsher realities of life. We see some indications of this in "September 1913," with lines like, "Romantic Ireland's dead and gone. It's with O'Leary in the grave." The cynicism intensifies as the years go by; the poetic melodies are forsaken as the dream fades. We see this directly in the simple little poem "A Coat."

Its small number of lines alone frankly reverses the purpose and style of Yeats' early poetry, and the poem could be said to refute directly the earlier "The Cloths of Heaven." "A Coat" needs little or no explanation:

> I made my song a coat
> Covered with embroideries
> Out of old mythologies
> From heel to throat;
> But the fools caught it,

Wore it in the world's eyes
As though they'd wrought it.
Song, let them take it,
For there's more enterprise
In walking naked.

In this tiny little poem Yeats puts aside the dreams he fashioned
from old Irish mythologies which suggested a more perfect world.
He now dedicates himself to focusing on the harder, more basic
realities of life. With the lines, "there's more enterprise in walking
naked," he gives up the embroidered cloth of old mythologies. The
lines in this poem are shorter, and the vocabulary is harder: many of
the words contain only one syllable—clipped and static. With the
cropped vocabulary, the short line, and the harder tone, the
rhythms are more abrupt as well—much more abrupt than, say, the
expansive lyricism in the embroidered cloths of gold and silver.

Another, more complicated and more interesting poem
deserves fuller attention for tensions inherent in it. "The Fisherman"
was written soon after "Easter 1916," which we have already discussed. Discursive and meditative, the poem is one of consolation.
In the first part Yeats speaks of his disappointment; in the second
part he consoles himself with a new thought, a new goal, to replace
the one that has dissolved. The opening lines of the poem introduce
an image typical of his earlier poetry, a fisherman, perhaps in Yeats'
County Sligo; it's a dream image and it now begins to grow dim.

Although I can see him still,
The freckled man who goes
To a grey place on a hill
In grey Connemara clothes
At dawn to cast his flies,
It's long since I began
To call up to the eyes
This wise and simple man.

This image from the past Yeats recognizes as a representation
of what he longed for.

All day I'd looked in the face
What I had hoped 'twould be
To write for my own race.

In Yeats' younger days he had hoped, as we know, to write poetry that embodied the Irish national spirit, an Irish national spirit which he found in a wise, simple, and ideally presented man who lived by casting his lot with the sea. The next lines reveal Yeats' growing cynicism as he recognizes that the concrete reality of Ireland differs quite markedly from the idealized form he used to give it. Hence, in the next, contrasting line—"And the reality"—Yeats lists the realities of contemporary Ireland that disenchant him or that operate to dissolve the dream:

> The living men that I hate,
> The dead man that I loved,

Many read this as a direct reference to John Synge, the author of "Riders to the Sea" and "Playboy of the Western World."

> The craven man in his seat,
> The insolent unreproved.

These lines may refer to the middle class as depicted in "September 1913." Yeats was increasingly disenchanted with the commercial class, especially after the lockout of Dublin workers in 1913.

> And no knave brought to book
> Who has won a drunken cheer,
> The witty man and his joke
> Aimed at the commonest ear.

Here Yeats again assesses the common people of Ireland, but this time as boring and ordinary, rather than as the inspired human beings that he had earlier depicted.

> The clever man who cries
> The catch cries of a clown,
> The beating down of the wise
> And the great Art beaten down.

A few years before this poem was written, you will remember Yeats' friend, Hugh Lane, wanted to give his collection of paintings to the City of Dublin if it would provide a proper museum for them. The city fathers, led by William Martin Murphy, leader of the Dublin lockout, voted not to accept the collection. This outraged Yeats because he regarded the paintings highly and believed they would bring cultural enrichment to Ireland. He felt keenly the difference between his values and those of the city fathers. Rejection of the paintings simply manifested Irish short-sightedness, a beating down of great art.

The poem contains two stanzas. Yeats acknowledges in the first that the image he had of Ireland — the simple fisherman — is no longer valid. Insolence, commonness, commercialism, and lack of culture now characterize the country. The second stanza creates a new image of the fisherman, or presents him in a different light, which yields up Yeats' solace as well. He begins the second stanza saying that almost a year has gone by since he began to create this new image:

> Maybe a twelvemonth since
> Suddenly I began,
> In scorn of this audience,
> Imagining a man,
> And his sun-freckled face
> And grey Connemara cloth,
> Climbing up to a place
> Where stone is dark under froth.

Notice in the later poetry that Yeats frequently perceives a need to lift oneself above the crowd. Yeats is creating his new image in scorn of his crass audience; Yeats becomes increasingly aristocratic as he grows older. Many times in the later poetry we find images of Yeats climbing higher, as the fisherman does in the poem. In fact, a later volume of poetry is even entitled *The Tower*. When Yeats married, he moved to Galway to live in an old tower, Thoor Ballylee, that he had rehabilitated. Another volume of poetry Yeats called *The Winding Stair*. Both volumes contain poems in which he climbs higher and higher to view life from an elevated position or to look down on it with a broader perspective and distanced objectivity. Yeats came to feel that age caused people to move out of the immersion of self in life, to detach themselves. They *watch* things happen rather than take part *in* what's happening. The suggestion of this elevation begins with this new image of the fisherman "climbing up to a place where stone is dark under froth,"

And the down-turn of his wrist
When the flies drop in the stream;
A man who does not exist,
A man who is but a dream.

He's a new dream, a presentation of Yeats' new relationship with, or at least his new attitude towards Ireland. The attitude becomes clearer in the last lines of the poem,

And cried, "Before I am old
I shall have written him one
Poem maybe as cold
And passionate as the dawn."

There is a puzzling tension between the word "cold" and the word "passionate." We tend to conceive them in opposition to one another. Many readers suggest that Yeats here constructs an image of Parnell as the aloof, somewhat forbidding, and, if you wish, somewhat cold man he appeared to be, with the air of nobility about him that made him an awesome and respectable figure. Yet that image was revealed to be only a partial portrait when revelation of his adulterous relationship uncloaked an unsuspected intensity of feeling and passion in Parnell. The tensions of Parnell as a passionate man concealed beneath a cold and forbidding exterior appealed to Yeats at this particular time.

Here Yeats will remain a passionate man, but he will curb revelation of passion as he becomes an aloof, cynical, forbidding man, a man who is in control. Hence he will appear cold. The control which causes him to appear cold must be strong because it must keep in check an inordinately intense passion. The image and the ideal for Yeats in the later period is of a man who feels, but who does not wear his heart on his sleeve, a man who keeps passion cloaked beneath a forbidding exterior. That forbidding exterior necessitates an enormous amount of discipline since it must control passion greater than that known by the common man. Hence the poem that Yeats would write, as he says at the end of "The Fisherman," will appear cold, abrupt, or cynical in tone, but only because it serves to curb or control the intensity of the poet's feeling. The internal intensities of Yeats' affection remain the same, but their expression changes. We no longer find lush rhythms and emotionally and sensually alluring lines of undulating soft rhythms. Instead Yeats chooses colder, harder images, but with passion encased in those harder rhythms.

Yeats has, of course, a conflict here between the cold and the passionate. Yeats wants to keep them in balance, as on a jeweler's scale with the trays on each side. One must be the equal of the other. The coldness must equal the passion, to keep it in check. And at the point of balance between coldness and passion stands Yeats. A continuing fascination with the point of balance fills Yeats' later verse. In "The Fisherman" Yeats expresses a neutral concern for balance. With equal weights in place, cold and passion are balanced, and that still point of neutrality becomes the central focus. In looking back over the poem, notice that Yeats repeats the neutral color gray. The Fisherman is in gray Connemara cloth; the stones are gray. Color is almost absent from the poem. This differs quite noticeably from the earlier poems with their many iridescent colors and gold and silver. Here the color is neutral, as the point of balance. Attaining a point of balance is an admirable thing for a human being; he is able to feel an intensity of passion but also to assert strength of self to hold in or control that passion.

It's beneficial, now, to read the poem as a whole.

Although I can see him still,
The freckled man who goes
To a grey place on a hill
In grey Connemara clothes
At dawn to cast his flies,
It's long since I began
To call up to the eyes
This wise and simple man.
All day I'd looked in the face
What I hoped 'twould be
To write for my own race
And the reality;
The living man that I hate,
The dead man that I loved,
The craven man in his seat,
The insolent unreproved,
And no knave brought to book
Who has won a drunken cheer,
The witty man and his joke

Aimed at the commonest ear,
The clever man who cries
The catch-cries of the clown,
The beating down of the wise
And great Art beaten down.

Maybe a twelvemonth since
Suddenly I began,
In scorn of this audience,
Imagining a man,
And his sun-freckled face,
And grey Connemara cloth,
Climbing up to a place
Where stone is dark under froth,
And the down-turn of his wrist
When the flies drop in the stream;
A man who does not exist,
A man who is but a dream;
And cried, "Before I am old
I shall have written him one
Poem maybe as cold
And passionate as the dawn."

In "Sailing to Byzantium," written in 1927 when Yeats was sixty-two years old, the poet turns his attention to age, time, and death. In "The Fisherman" he mentions age — "Before I am old/I shall have written him one/Poem maybe as cold/And passionate as the dawn." Yeats was always very aware of time passing and of his own age. Even as a young man he worried about growing old and the relentlessness of time. In the last years of his life, when Yeats knew he was dying, he spent his time rereading his poems for a final volume of his collected verse. He recognized then that the continuing major theme of his poetry was a concern for and an opposition to the relentlessness of time and death and the inevitability of death. As he grew older this opposition to time and death intensified and his own assertions of life in opposition to time and death strengthened.

In early poems like "The Stolen Child" we tended to hear the beautiful, escapist yearning to leave this world of time and go to a permanent, more perfect world, the land of the faery, because "the world's more full of weeping" as one of the repeated lines in the poem says. But the lines themselves are calm and smooth. In later poems like "Sailing to Byzantium" Yeats states his struggle against time and death in a more grasping and complicated way. He presents his thoughts and his desires in a less emotional and more intellectual form. The imagery is harder. His agonized passion is controlled by and expressed through more brittle, more academic images, and with more complicated reasoning. "Sailing to Byzantium" is a great work of literature, and as with many great works, its depths and its complexities arouse continuing reverberations. The poem rewards careful attention.

Yeats uses the city of Byzantium as his own individual and personal symbol. Byzantium, once called Constantinople, now known as Istanbul, has gone through a number of name changes. It's a significant city for America because when the Turks overran Constantinople, they closed it to European travelers, who prior to that had gone through Constantinople on their way to the Orient. Because of this Christopher Columbus sailed westward, trying to find a new route to the east, and landed in America. But Byzantium is an interesting city for a number of other reasons. It stands partially in Europe and partially in Asia; it straddles two continents. It's part western and part eastern. It's a beautiful city scenically. In the manner of San Francisco in the United States the city sits on land cut by waterways. Rising up from these waterways are sloping hills, so that, as in San Francisco, wherever you stand, a beautiful vista of water and land and the towers of the city opens up before you. Myriads of domed churches and mosques make the city even more beautiful and interesting. The most famous of those churches and mosques are the larger ones — Santa Sophia, the Blue Mosque, and the Mosque of Sulieman the Magnificent — but there are hundreds of smaller ones. Hence, when you stand on the hillside in Istanbul, it seems that the domes are floating on the horizon. Those airborne towers form part of Yeats' imagery. The Byzantium that Yeats envisions in the poem is the city in the fifth and sixth centuries, just before the reign of Emperor Justinian.

Yeats thought that "in early Byzantium, maybe never before or since in recorded history, religious, aesthetic, and practical life were one." Yeats felt that there the ordinary populace were at once artists as well as ordinary people, that each lived in a world that was practical but that was also infused with cultural and aesthetic sensibility. Every individual lived in cultural awareness at the same time that he worked with his hands as an artisan.

Very likely Yeats was influenced by the Victorian writer
William Morris in his admiration for the artistic craftsman. While
production lines and mechanized manufacturing had not taken over
yet, William Morris anticipated their effect. In modern life Morris
saw that an ordinary citizen might have a job in, say, a furniture
factory, where his task might be to make over and over one leg for
desks that were being turned out by the hundreds or the thousands.
This man would stand in place making one leg, then another, then
another. In a day of work his job would become repetitious and boring—certainly not satisfying to his spirit or his creativity. Morris
wanted the individual to fashion his own desk from start to finish.
He would select the wood from whatever trees were
available—maple, butternut, mahogany. He would cut down the
tree, prepare and season the wood. Then he would design the
desk—decide how big it was to be, what design he would like, and
how it would fit into the house. And then he would actually make it,
join the wood, hand carve the decorations, stain it as he chose, and
bring it to the level of finish he preferred. When the desk was finished, the person who made it, this ordinary human being, would
feel personal satisfaction and pride in his work and would know that
he had contributed to its creation. He would have shaped the desk,
almost like a work of art, and he would feel aesthetic satisfaction in
its beauty. The man in the furniture factory, to the contrary, merely
makes leg after leg after leg, feeling no pride or aesthetic satisfaction
in his work.

Yeats suggested that in Byzantium just before the reign of
Justinian ordinary people doing their everyday work were, at the
same time, performing aesthetically. They were being human in the
full sense of the term. Their feelings and artistic sensibilities could
find expression in their everyday performances. Life in the nineteenth or twentieth centuries, however, was fragmenting, and
human beings no longer had the same opportunity to express their
aesthetic sensibilities. Hence, for Yeats Byzantium has particular
meaning as a place where a practical world and a beautiful world
are one, united into a single reality.

The desire for this unity recalls that expressed in Yeats' early
poems. In "The Stolen Child" when the child goes off to the faery
world, Yeats laments that the child no longer will hear the cows lowing on the hillside or the teakettle humming softly on the fire. What
Yeats wanted in "The Stolen Child" was to combine all the benefits

of the faery world with all the benefits of the real world in one place. And he couldn't.

Yeats imagined that Byzantium perfectly joined the real world and the perfect world, the practical world and the aesthetic world. But we should turn to the poem itself to see what it says in its own right, and how it communicates the intensity of passion and feeling that Yeats was experiencing at this later stage in his life. The poem reads:

That is no country for old men. The young
In one another's arms, birds in the trees
—Those dying generations—at their song,
The salmon-falls, the mackerel-crowded seas,
Fish, flesh, or fowl, commend all summer long
Whatever is begotten, born, and dies.
Caught in that sensual music all neglect
Monuments of unageing intellect.

An aged man is but a paltry thing,
A tattered coat upon a stick, unless
Soul clap its hands and sing, and louder sing
For every tatter in its mortal dress,
Nor is there singing school but studying
Monuments of its own magnificence;
And therefore I have sailed the seas and come
To the holy city of Byzantium.

O sages standing in God's holy fire
As in the gold mosaic of a wall,
Come from the holy fire, perne in a gyre,
And be the singing-masters of my soul.
Consume my heart away; sick with desire
And fastened to a dying animal
It knows not what it is; and gather me
Into the artifice of eternity.

Once out of nature I shall never take
My bodily form from any natural thing,
But such a form as Grecian goldsmiths make
Of hammered gold and gold enamelling
To keep a drowsy Emperor awake;
Or set upon a golden bough to sing
To lords and ladies of Byzantium
Of what is past, or passing, or to come.

The poem opens with a rather abrupt sentence—"That is no country for old men." The pronoun "that" refers ahead to what is in the stanza. The country that he no longer feels at home in is a country in which the young are in one another's arms. The "birds in the trees—those dying generations—at their song, the salmon-falls, the mackerel-crowded seas, flesh, or fowl, commend all summer long whatever is begotten, born, and dies."

These images tend to be sensual images, or images dealing with the communication of the sensual, physical, or emotional. The young in one another's arms is the first indication of that sensuality. The others are less sharp. Salmon have an extraordinary urge when it comes time for spawning; all salmon struggle to go back to where they were born to spawn the next generation. So intense is their instinct that they can swim against the current in strong rivers and can leap up waterfalls to get back to the place from which they came.

In these lines Yeats deliberately includes creatures from all of nature's realms—the birds from the air, the fish from the water, and human beings from the land. In all parts of life—sky, sea, and earth—sensual music sings of being begotten, being born, and then dying. There is a physical and sensual rhythm in life; the cycle inevitably comes to death.

In the last lines of the stanza, Yeats states clearly the problem, that humans, caught in that sensual music, "Neglect monuments of unageing intellect." While everything in life seems to change, to alter, to grow old, and to die, there are some things that do not. These are monuments that represent the intellectual rather than the transitory emotional. Hence, one sees that the country that is not for an old man is a country dealing with feeling, emotion, or the sensual rhythms of life. The country that is meant for an older person is one in which the unageing intellect can communicate with things that do not change. That's a country for an old man, not one in which the people are still caught in sensual music. So Yeats says in the next stanza, he's leaving and sailing to Byzantium, a place that for him holds monuments of unageing intellect. The second stanza focuses attention on old age. The opening two lines illustrate the harder, sharper tone and rhythm in the later Yeats. The spare images reflect his emotional intensity:

An aged man is but a paltry thing,
A tattered coat upon a stick,

Quite a different tone and rhythm from the lush and beautiful rhythms and scenes of the early Yeats. The clipped and simple vocabulary and the sharp images reveal contained emotion.

The word "unless," which follows, introduces the next idea of the poem, that an aged man is but a paltry thing, *unless* "soul clap its hands and sing." Here we have the contrast of body and soul, the body being the sensual and the emotional element that dies, the soul being an immortal essence. The soul can continue to live and "clap its hands, . . . and louder sing for every tatter in its mortal dress." The older the person gets, the more tattered and ragged the body, the more vibrant can be the soul. In this antithetical ratio, as body grows weaker, the soul grows stronger. The soul, of course, is what perceives and responds to the monuments of unageing intellect; the body is what has responded to the sensual music. In the next lines, "Nor is there singing school but studying monuments of its own magnificence; and therefore I have sailed the seas and come to the holy city of Byzantium," Yeats announces the holy city of Byzantium as the city filled with monuments of unageing splendor, the place for an old man. There the soul can be in touch with those of others, particularly other artists — the implication being that as an artist molds and shapes his work, that part of himself is in it and is communicated to others through it. In Byzantium Yeats' soul can communicate with, or be taught by, spirits that are inherent in the works of art that are in the city of Byzantium.

Byzantium's art is of a particular kind. Perhaps its most famous form is the mosaic, pictures composed with tiny squares or pieces of tile made from clay, shaped, baked, painted, and fired so that the paint, often gold enamel, has a smooth, hard surface. Each tile is skillfully put into plaster or cement in a wall or dome to form a final image, frequently the portrait of a saint. The mosaic is a work of art, hard and permanent.

As Yeats looks for a monument of unageing intellect, something that is permanent and defies time, he selects, in Byzantine art, an image of an art form that is by its very nature enduring. Enriching the meaning of the poem, the mosaics in Byzantine art originate in ordinary clay; the ordinary is raised to the permanent; the mortal becomes immortal. The dirt of earth passes through various shapings and firings; ordinary clay becomes extraordinary art.

The third stanza of the poem, a somewhat more complicated

one, suggests a particular kind of Byzantine work of art, depictions of saints or sages.

> O sages standing in God's holy fire
> As in the gold mosaic of a wall.

One could interpret the lines as describing the actual pictures of the saints, who are indeed standing in fire, or have fire around their feet—fires of fortune or of divine love—not unlikely ways to depict the saints. Or one might read the lines as describing the reflections from the gold of the mosaic as it sparkles, or flashes. Or, thirdly, one could think of the lines as describing both the finished artistic portrait of the saints on the wall and the process of firing of the pieces of the mosaic to produce the hardened surfaces of the tiles. Indeed, the portrayal of the saints did come from a fire, a fire that is an artistically holy one, from Yeats' point of view, because what it has purified is ordinary earth. Having been purified by the fire, the clay can serve to portray saints. And Yeats wants the saints to teach him, since he said in the earlier stanza that he was going to Byzantium to have his soul taught in a singing school of monuments of unageing intellect. Here, by standing before one of these monuments of unageing intellect, his own soul is to be enlarged and enlightened. This is satisfaction for an old man. The sages on the wall are coming from holy fire to be the singing masters of his soul.

In the phrase "perne in a gyre," the word gyre, the root word of gyroscope, means, as Yeats uses it, an ever-increasing spiral. It's another of those ascending images we spoke of before, like the spiral staircase or the tower. Here something is emerging or surfacing at the top of the spiral. The term perne is an archaic word meaning a bobbin—like the spool in a sewing machine—something that turns around. The depiction of the saints has emerged out of the whirl or spiral of life. The spiral itself is conical and has its base point. When you wash dishes and there are little pieces of lettuce in the dishwater, when you open the drain, the water spirals around and gurgles down the drain. As it does, the lettuce floats to the top of the water as it's going down, lifted by the force of the spiraling water. The lettuce will float on top, while the water continues to swirl. The laws of physics dictate that while the spiral keeps going down, what's inside rises to the top. Out of the energy of the spiral's action something floats, is exuded, or emerges. For Yeats, out of all the energies of the cycles of life — out of whatever is begotten, lives, and dies — something emerges as permanent essence. Out of all the cycles of earthly existence in Byzantium comes this depiction of the sages on this wall, as a monument of unageing intellect, as a permanent thing, that has emerged like a perne in a gyre, and now is teaching the spirit or the soul of Yeats.

He asks the sages, "Consume my heart away." The heart is, of course, a representation of the sensual or the bodily. Yeats would like to subdue the body so that his soul can be released from its attachment to the body:

> Consume my heart away; sick with desire
> And fastened to a dying animal
> It knows not what it is.

Yeats wants his soul released from the body so that it can find its identity with the immortal sages in eternity: "gather me into the artifice of eternity." He carefully uses the word *artifice* rather than the word *art*, because *artifice* implies the hand work of the ordinary person in Byzantium making the work of art.

Another time in history Yeats might have chosen, and it's interesting he didn't, was the Middle Ages, the centuries in which ordinary citizens made magnificent cathedrals, filled with beautiful pieces of art — carved stone, stained glass, and carved wood wrought by the common man. Probably Yeats deliberately avoided the Western Christian image as too narrow and not suiting his own inclinations.

In the last stanza Yeats suggests the kind of artistic form he wishes his soul to take when it is released:

> Once out of nature I shall never take
> My bodily form from any natural thing,
> But such a form as Grecian goldsmiths make
> Of hammered gold and gold enamelling
> To keep a drowsy Emperor awake;

Once a friend of Yeats asked him what he specifically meant in those lines. He said he had once been told that a Byzantine emperor had had a tree made all out of gold in his palace, and on the tree were little golden birds which sang, probably with music boxes inside of them. The birds were so carefully made that they appeared to be singing. A golden bird, at least in this stage of Yeats' life, would be preferable to a living bird. The living bird, with blood and flesh in a world of time, was not as beautiful or as permanent as the artistic, solid, golden bird. For Yeats the real bird was important only in that it provided an artist with a model from which he could then shape, according to his own feeling, the golden bird. The living bird would just die, but the golden bird became a permanent artifice of eternity. Hence, in the poem Yeats hopes that after he dies his spirit will take some other form. He will be transformed, he hopes, into something like a golden bird; he wants reincarnation not as anything mortal or natural, nothing with flesh, but as something permanent like a golden bird "to keep a drowsy Emperor awake; or set upon a golden bough to sing to the lords and ladies of Byzantium of what is past, or passing, or to come." Only the golden bird goes on; it is eternal, always part of the past, part of the present, part of the future.

The poem betrays mortal pain at the loss of the physical self and simultaneously expresses Yeats' intense desire to assure himself of an eternal permanence for his own spirit. It's his assertion of self over the realities of death. The poem, phrased in simple language, expresses complex thought as it reasons out, perhaps in a desperate way, a reality of eternity of self in art. Though the images are concrete or hard images, unlike those in such earlier poems as the "Wandering Aengus," we still see Yeats' aesthetic sensibility. Remember these are golden birds. In the earlier poems he gave us the silver apples of the moon, the golden apples of the sun, or the embroidered cloths of heaven. Yeats' attachment to things of aesthetic beauty remains even though it finds a different mode of expression.

The poem has its desperate passion. Its reasoning and its hard images control the intensity of its feeling. It is a poem as cold and as passionate as the dawn, the goal Yeats set himself in "The Fisherman." And it is a poem that once again reflects Yeats' double vision of an eternal, spiritual world, and a tangible, concrete world. The real world of time overwhelmed Yeats in 1939. He died in southern France and was buried there because the war prevented bringing his body back to Ireland. After the war his body was returned to the earth of Sligo. He was buried in a cemetery near the mountain that was for him, and for many in the past, the home of mythological Irish spirits, the mountain called Ben Bulben.

In his last poem, entitled "Under Ben Bulben," Yeats provided

23. Yeats' grave in Drumcliffe, County Sligo, "under Ben Bulben," the mountain cited in Yeats' poems. (See picture, p. 88) (Irish Tourist Board)

his own epitaph, which is carved on the simple hard slab that marks his grave. The poetic lines once again reveal his advice to balance life and death with controlled neutrality. The last lines give advice to a horseman who, riding by this graveyard, might stop to look at the grave of Yeats. They suggest that the horseman should look carefully on the fact of life, look carefully on the fact of death, put them together with a balanced outlook, and then go on. The tombstone of Yeats has the epitaph,

> Cast a cold eye
> On life, on death.
> Horseman, pass by!

24. The front of a small working-class house in Dublin.

CHAPTER TEN

Dubliners

D UBLIN, AS THE major city and the capital of Ireland, represents the nation. first-time travellers to Ireland never pass it by, but they may be wisely advised to tour the countryside first to better understand what seems at first Dublin's shabbiness and to accept the city as the urban manifestation and life center of the small, essentially rural nation it represents. Now that we have seen Irish country life in literature, we can approach Dublin and its presentation in literature.

Dublin is basically an eighteenth-century city in its plan and primary architecture. In the eighteenth century it was second only to London in the British Isles. After the defeat of James II in 1690 in the Battle of the Boyne, the English proceeded with confidence to build what was sometimes called the "Queen City of the Empire." Dublin became in time a city of some wealth and fashion. The Irish labor supply, an inexpensive one, helped build and maintain the city, just as it built and supplied the big houses in the countryside, houses described in *Castle Rackrent.*

Dublin was developed in an orderly, reasonable way, typical of the eighteenth century, the Age of Reason. The city plan exhibits a classical sense of order. Intersected by a river, the Liffey, the city was built along both shores. At right angles to the river is Dublin's main street, now called O'Connell Street. The outer limits of the city were then enclosed by a canal; a circular road was later built along that canal. Much of the inner part of the city followed a grid plan, with squares of houses that often enclosed parks at their center. A large park, St. Stephen's Green, dominated the smaller squares.

25. The Customs House along the River Liffey, one of Dublin's several buildings of classical architecture. (Irish Tourist Board)

The major buildings were classical in style, built by significant architects of the period. The Customs House, the Four Courts building, and the Bank of Ireland building stand in present-day Dublin as examples of the monumental style of the period's architecture.

Residential streets were lined with Georgian houses with simple flat brick fronts, large windows and handsome doorways, usually with brass appointments and archways with fan windows over them. The upper class Ascendancy lived here, while the Irish poor tucked themselves into small shelters in dark rambling alleyways, similar to those we have touched on in *Strumpet City*.

But, of course, the main thing that makes a city and contributes to its personality is its people. We've already encountered a broad spectrum of social and intellectual classes in Dublin—the city's working class in O'Casey's "The Plough and the Stars" and the full panorama of people in *Strumpet City*. O'Casey drew yet another

26. The Four Courts, another Dublin building of classical architecture along the Liffey. (Irish Tourist Board)

portrait of the working class in a play entitled "Juno and the Paycock." His sympathy with them and his respect for their zest and endurance are clearly evident.

But for literature about Dublin we can do no better than James Joyce's fine collection of short stories, *Dubliners*. The book presents a unique collection of stories about middle-class Dublin life early in this century. Filled with details of everyday, these stories taken all together provide a comprehensive picture of Dublin life at the turn of the century — and perhaps still for some. Joyce had removed himself from the developing Irish literary movement and its idealistic nationalism, and with *Dubliners* tried to show the reality of Ireland without hallucinations. In many ways his book is a criticism of Irish society, with the focal character in each story representing a particular aspect of it. Hence the stories are at once realistic and symbolic.

The order of the stories in the volume is important, as Joyce

27. A row of Georgian houses in Merrion Square, Dublin. (Irish Tourist Board)

28. The doorway of a Georgian house, with its classical pillars and fan window.

made clear: "My intention was to write a chapter of the moral history of my country. . . . I have tried to present it to the indifferent public under its four aspects: childhood, adolescence, maturity and public life." The order of the stories reflects this. The first two stories deal with childhood; the third story, "Araby," with adolsecence. All three are told from the young person's point of view:the child or the adolescent actually tells the story. The next eight stories tell about "mature" people. The main characters are old enough to be physically mature, though Joyce certainly questions how emotionally or psychologically mature they are. These eight stories fall into four pairs of stories dealing with particular aspects of mature life. "Eveline" and "After The Race" deal with family life. "Two Gallants" and "The Boarding House" deal with dominance — male dominance in "Two Gallants" and female dominance in "The Boarding House." The next pair, "A Little Cloud" and "Counterparts," focuses on the frustration of males in normal life. The last two stories consider celibates, a female celibate in "Clay" and a male celibate in "A Painful Case."

After these stories of childhood, adolescence and maturity, Joyce turns in the next three stories to aspects of what he called "public life." These public concerns are political, cultural, and religious: "Ivy Day In The Committee Room" deals with the discussions preceding the vote to unseat Parnell; "A Mother" concerns a mother's embarrasing smallmindedness as she pushes her daughter into a concert, and "Grace" focuses on the behind-the-scenes connivances of friends and family attempting to get an ailing, drinking man to attend a mission — a series of sermons and religious observances designed to restore one's devotion and faith. The collection of stories concludes with a story Joyce added later — a long, complex, and important work entitled "The Dead." When Joyce added "The Dead" to *Dubliners*, he said that in the previous stories "it seems to me that I have been unnecessarily harsh. I have reproduced none of the attractiveness of the city. . . . I have not reproduced its ingenuous insularity and its hospitality. . . . I have not been just to its beauty." Joyce was, of course, pointedly critical in the earlier stories. How much compensation he offers, whether he presents Dublin's attractiveness, hospitality, and beauty in "The Dead" is left for the individual reader to decide.

While the stories in the volume are held together by order and organization, they are also united by the recurrent pattern of each story and by a specific repetition of the overall thematic concern about the paralysis that affects Ireland. In each of the stories we find a main character or characters caught, trapped, imprisoned, or paralyzed—usually by their own psychological incapacities, incapacities stemming from continually repressive forces in Dublin and in Irish society. The works concentrate on a psychological paralysis; each story builds to the exposure or recognition of that psychological paralysis either by the character himself, as in "Araby" and "The Dead," by other characters in the story, as in "Clay," or by the reader only, as in "Two Gallants." Each story begins easily, almost innocently, with small details narrated in a seemingly drifting way—until, at the end of the story, the details fall into place and with their cumulative effect we see fully the complete reality—the facts of the situation and the surrounding psychological environment. The moment of recognition thus created Joyce called the epiphany of the story, the word epiphany meaning revelation. In the stories there is often a character who, at the beginning of the story, longs for something: to play hookey from school for a day and go on an adventure, to satisfy a "crush" on a girl by buying her a gift at a carnival, to attain an important, worldly job in a big city, to have a husband, a wife. By the end of the story the person doesn't get satisfaction or attain or obtain what he or she yearned for, and the reader sees why: the psychological inabilities or paralysis within the character himself or herself has caused the defeat. There is, in the stories, continuing frustration, corruption, and decay. All want to escape; none succeed.

The story "Eveline" is an effective, representative illustration. The story, one in the "maturity" group, deals with family, a particularly noteworthy Irish concern. It opens with Eveline sitting at the window, watching evening invade the avenue, thinking of the changes over the past years and the fact that she is the one "child" of the family to remain at home to care—bored and frustrated—for her widower father. Even her younger brother has gone off to a job. The father himself is demanding and often erupts into threats and violence. But Eveline has met Frank, a "kind, manly, open-hearted" person. She has been seeing him secretly—afraid to tell her father because she feels guilty of betraying him, and, perhaps, the responsibility left to her by the family. Frank is a sailor who started out as a deck boy but now has a good job in far-off Buenos Aires, Argentina; he wants Eveline to marry him and go to Buenos Aires to settle. She

29. A post-eighteenth century terrace of houses in Dublin.

secretly plans to do so, and to leave a note for her father when she leaves. As she thinks at the window of her mother's dreary life, she vividly imagines the step she plans to take with Frank:

> Frank would save her. He would give her life, perhaps love, too. But she wanted to live. Why should she be unhappy? She had a right to happiness. Frank would take her in his arms, fold her in his arms. He would save her.

The story then moves to its end, with Eveline at the station after she has left her farewell note at home.

> She stood among the swaying crowd in the station at the North Wall. He held her hand and she knew that he was speaking to her, saying something about the passage over and over again. The station was full of soldiers with brown baggages. Through the wide doors of the sheds she caught a glimpse of the black mass of the boat, lying beside the quay wall, with illumined portholes. She answered nothing. She felt her cheek pale and cold and, out of a maze of distress, she prayed to God to direct her, to show her what was her duty. The boat blew a long mournful whistle into the mist. If she went, to-morrow she would be on the sea with Frank, steaming towards Buenos Ayres. Their passage had been booked. Could she still draw back after all he had done for her? Her distress awoke a nausea in her body and she kept moving her lips in silent fervent prayer.
>
> A bell clanged upon her heart. She felt him seize her hand:
> "Come!"
>
> All the seas of the world tumbled about her heart. He was drawing her into them: he would drown her. She gripped with both hands at the iron railing.
> "Come!"
>
> No! No! No! It was impossible. Her hands clutched the iron in frenzy. Amid the seas she sent a cry of anguish!
> "Eveline! Evvy!"
>
> He rushed beyond the barrier and called to her to follow. He was shouted at to go on but he still called to her. She set her white face to him, passive, like a helpless animal. Her eyes gave him no sign of love or farewell or recognition.

Eveline is held back by her own ingrained psychological incapacity, by her own guilt. Joyce presents her standing, gripping the iron bars of the fence as a visible symbol of her less visible prison in the forces current in Dublin life.

This, then, is a representative story in what Joyce called his chapter of the moral history of his country. He felt and depicted the repressions in Ireland—particularly in Dublin as the capital and center of Ireland—repressions that he himself struggled to escape. Unlike Eveline, he left Ireland, but he wrote about it for the rest of his life, perhaps not having "escaped" after all.

Each of the three stories on public life builds to a moment of epiphany or revelation, but the revelation does not penetrate into the psychological condition of an individual character, but exposes the apparent realities, for Joyce the shabby and small-minded realities, of dominant elements of public life—culture, politics, and religion. "Ivy Day in the Committee Room," the political story, traces some of the tangential small talk and the small-mindedness of Dubliners' discussions at the meeting to vote on whether to continue supporting Parnell's leadership after his adulterous affair comes to light.

In "A Mother," the story about cultural life, Joyce portrays a mother arguing unpleasantly to the penny over the fee her daughter will receive for singing at a concert. The name of the concert manager, Mr. Holohan, is Joyce's ironic play on Yeats' idealistic personification of Ireland in "Cathleen ni Houlihan." For Joyce the cultural life in Ireland is seamy and penurious; it concerns itself with triviality and drowns itself in pettiness. This is the picture he presents in "A Mother."

"Grace" approaches the religious life of the Dubliners in the same mode. In this story the focal character, Mr. Kernan, is a frequent drunk who neglects to come home on time to his family, particularly on pay day. As the story begins, the drunken Mr. Kernan has just fallen down the stairs leading to the men's room and injured himself. When he is carried home by some friends, Mrs. Kernan is embarrassed that she has nothing in the house to feed to the friends who have brought her husband home. "We were waiting for him to come home with the money. He never seems to think he has a home at all," she says. These circumstances set in motion the main action of the story: the careful connivance of Mr. Kernan's friends and his wife to get Mr. Kernan to attend a retreat—a concentrated series of sermons and church ceremonies intended to revivify religious intensity. Mr. Kernan, a convert to Catholicism at his marriage, would

not be inclined to attend—he hasn't been to church in twenty
years—so he must be drawn by an oblique method, with the matter
carefully brought into casual conversation by his friends, Mr. Cunningham, Mr. M'Coy, and Mr. Power, when they visit Kernan, in bed
recovering from his fall. One scene presents their clever opening of
the subject:

> The gentlemen drank from their glasses, set the glasses again on
> the table and paused. Then Mr. Cunningham turned towards Mr.
> Power and said casually:
> —On Thursday night, you said, Jack?
> —Thursday, yes, said Mr. Power.
> —Righto! said Mr. Cunningham promptly.
> —We can meet in M'Auley's, said Mr. M'Coy. That'll be the
> most convenient place.
> —But we mustn't be late, said Mr. Power earnestly, because it
> is sure to be crammed to the doors.
> —We can meet a half-seven, said Mr. M'Coy.
> —Righto! said Mr. Cunningham.
> —Half-seven at M'Auley's be it!
> There was a short silence. Mr. Kernan waited to see whether he
> would be taken into his friend's confidence. Then he asked:
> —What's in the wind?
> —O, it's nothing, said Mr. Cunningham. It's only a little matter
> that we're arranging for Thursday.
> —The opera, is it? said Mr. Kernan.
> —No, no, said Mr. Cunningham in an evasive tone, it's just a lit-
> tle . . . spiritual matter.
> —O, said Mr. Kernan.
> There was silence again. Then Mr. Power said, point blank:
> —To tell you the truth, Tom, we're going to make a retreat.
> —Yes, that's it, said Mr. Cunningham, Jack and I and M'Coy
> here—we're all going to wash the pot.
> He uttered the metaphor with a certain homely energy and, en-
> couraged by his own voice, proceeded:
> —You see, we may as well all admit we're a nice collection of
> scoundrels, one and all. I say, one and all, he added with gruff
> charity and turning to Mr. Power. Own up now!
> —I own up, said Mr. Power.
> —And I own up, said Mr. M'Coy.
> —So we're going to wash the pot together, said Mr. Cun-
> ningham.

A thought seemed to strike him. He turned suddenly to the invalid and said:

—Do you know what, Tom, has just occurred to me? You might join in and we'd have four-handed reel.

—Good idea said Mr. Power. The four of us together.

Thus is Mr. Kernan set up. The men's conversation then turns to the superiority of the Jesuit order, the infallibility of the Pope when he speaks *ex cathedra*, and Catholicism as *the* one true religion. When Mrs. Kernan enters, Mr. Power says with "abrupt joviality,"

—Well, Mrs. Kernan, we're going to make your man a good holy pious and God-fearing Roman Catholic.

He swept his arm round the company inclusively.

—We're all going to make a retreat together and confess our sins—and God knows we want it badly.

—I don't mind, said Mr. Kernan, smiling a little nervously.

Mrs. Kernan thought it would be wiser to conceal her satisfaction. So she said:

—I pity the poor priest that has to listen to your tale.

Thus the operation of "grace" catches Mr. Kernan to go to the retreat; the story then shifts to the church itself. As the men wait for the ceremonies to begin, Mr. Cunningham points out to Mr. Kernan some of the people he thinks notable who are also in attendance: Mr. Harford, the moneylender; Michael Grimes, owner of three pawnshops, and some other "able, commercial" figures and politicians. The words of the priest's sermon are not included in the story. Rather, Joyce chose to describe it to highlight its commercial metaphor. The priest:

told his hearers that he was there that evening for no terrifying, no extravagant purpose; but as a man of the world speaking to his fellow-men. He came to speak to businessmen and he would speak to them in a businesslike way. If he might use the metaphor, he said, he was their spiritual accountant; and he wished each and every one of his hearers to open his books, the books of his spiritual life, and see if they tallied accurately with conscience. . . . But one thing only, he said, he would ask of his hearers. And that was: to be straight and manly with God. If their accounts tallied in every point to say:

—Well, I have verified my accounts. I find all well.

But if, as might happen, there were some discrepancies, to admit the truth, to be frank and say like a man:

— Well, I have looked into my accounts. I find this wrong and this wrong. But, with God's grace, I will rectify this and this. I will set right my accounts.

Thus, as the story closes, Joyce reveals or exposes the religious life of middle-class Dublin, with spiritual life and God's grace ignominiously and distastefully reduced to a ledger of financial accounts. The religious spirit of the people, just like their cultural and political life and their individual psychological capacities, is imprisoned, in this case by provinciality and a commercial mentality. Their aspirations are held in or limited by a shabby, small-mindedness. The public life of the Dubliners is as narrow and inept as their individual lives. For Joyce, the repressions in Ireland are widespread.

30. An Irish boy on the farm.

CHAPTER ELEVEN

Joyce and McGahern

IRISH AUTHORS and the Irish people in general are often concerned about the past, frequently the distant past. We've seen many authors whose interest reaches back to Irish mythological times. Other Irish authors concentrate on the more immediate past. And a number of authors write about their own individual pasts, their own upbringings, their childhood. Both James Joyce, in *A Portrait of the Artist as a Young Man*, and John McGahern, in his novel *The Dark*, focus on growing up in Ireland. As we give our attention to growing up in Ireland, it will help to recall briefly other works we have discussed.

Synge's "Playboy of the Western World" gave us insight into the life of the boy with the tyrannical father. In "Riders To The Sea," the play in which all of Maurya's sons drown, we see the very real hazards that threaten the life of the young men of the islands. A number of stories in *Dubliners* provide insights into childhood experiences. "The Sisters" tells about a little boy going to the wake of his friend, an aged priest; in "An Encounter," the boys play hookey from school to have a bit of an adventure; and in "Araby," a young lad has a crush on the girl across the street. Even some of the stories which don't focus on childhood shed light on it. In the story "Little Cloud," a baby has a weak and ineffective father, which bodes ill for the child's future. In "Counterparts," a big Irishman comes home after being defeated at work and in the bar, and his little boy tries to prevent his father's beating him by offering a prayer. While these latter are vignettes only, they add breadth to our consideration. In this regard we should not overlook O'Flaherty's story "Going Into Exile," and the emotional uprooting of the young people in that story as they prepare to emigrate to the United States.

But we will first focus on Joyce's masterful novel, *A Portrait of the Artist as a Young Man*. The novel is a complex one that has generated continuing high praise and a sizable number of interpretations and scholarly articles. We will not even attempt to examine the book comprehensively, but will look at how the novel reflects the experience of a child growing up in Ireland. The novel is autobiographical, and the child is, in many ways, Joyce.

Born and raised in Dublin, Joyce experienced an ordinary, Dublin, middle-class childhood, but we must always remember that Joyce himself was not ordinary. No one doubts that Joyce was a literary genius, but he was also an intellectual one, with great mental abilities and breadth of knowledge. Part of the book's complexities arise because an extraordinary boy was raised in an ordinary way in Ireland; the book describes his feelings of being repressed by certain aspects of ordinary Irish life.

We saw an early indication of Joyce's concern about the repressive forces in society in *Dubliners*; a number of characters in those stories are incapacitated by the society in which they live.

While *A Portrait of the Artist as a Young Man* contains many details of daily life, the novel essentially examines an interior reality. While it portrays exterior reality in detail, its essence concerns the interior thoughts and the interior consciousness of the main character, Stephen Dedalus. Joyce chose this name very carefully.

The first name, Stephen, recalls the first Christian martyr, whose feast day in Christian liturgy falls on December 26th. The surname, Dedalus, recalls the character named Dedalus in Greek mythology, who, wanting to fly, made functioning wings by molding wax and affixing feathers. He flew successfully. (His son, Icarus, however, doing likewise, flew too close to the sun, which melted the wax and destroyed the wings; Icarus fell to earth.) Joyce's use of the name of Dedalus for the main character of the novel suggests a soaring hope, a desire to fly, to escape. The urge to escape from the aspects of everyday life in Dublin that Joyce presents in the novel develops in the mind of Stephen Dedalus. Escape becomes a major theme.

The novel takes place in the mind of Stephen. His mind unfolds as he discovers and grows throughout this childhood. Through the experiences of early days he arrives at decisions or conclusions about himself or about life in general. Joyce carefully counterpoints these discoveries with the scenes from daily life which lead to the discoveries and the decisions.

The novel begins when Stephen is so young that the first paragraph may put a reader off it is so childlike:

> Once upon a time and a very good time it was there was a moocow coming down along the road and this moocow that was coming down along the road met a nicens little boy named baby tuckoo. . . .
>
> His father told him that story: his father looked at him through a glass: he had a hairy face.
>
> He was baby tuckoo. The moocow came down the road where Betty Bryne lived: she sold lemon platt.
>
> *"O, the wild rose blossoms*
> *On the little green place."*
>
> He sang that song. That was his song.
>
> *Oh, the green wothe botheth.*
>
> When you wet the bed first it is warm then it gets cold. His mother put on the oilsheet. That had the queer smell.
>
> His mother had a nicer smell than his father. She played on the piano the sailor's hornpipe for him to dance.

And so it goes. You see the interior thoughts of the leading character, here a baby.

The book rather quickly moves to scenes in school, which stress the severity of some of the teachers. In one incident Stephen has broken his glasses. The teacher doesn't believe that Stephen has broken his glasses accidentally and that he shouldn't read without them. The teacher thinks it's a ploy to avoid school work. When the prefect of studies arrives in the classroom he too doesn't believe Stephen's explanation. He decides to punish Stephen as an example to the other boys and to Stephen. The punishment is physical, apparently a usual form of discipline at that time in Irish schools. Some of us may have memories of similar incidents in our own training in the United States. But Joyce never forgot the punishment; this childhood event helped to form his adult attitude evident in the novel.

The scene begins with the prefect of studies speaking as he enters the classroom:

> You, boy, who are you?
> Stephen's heart jumped suddenly.
> —Dedalus, sir.
> —Why are you not writing like the others?
> —I . . . my . . ., He could not speak with fright.

—Why is he not writing. Father Arnall?

—He broke his glasses said Father Arnall and I exempted him from work.

—Broke? What is this I hear? What is this your name is? said the prefect of studies.

—Dedalus, sir.

—Out here, Dedalus. Lazy little schemer. I see schemer in your face. Where did you break your glasses?

Stephen stumbled into the middle of the class, blinded by fear and haste.

—Where did you break your glasses? repeated the prefect of studies.

—The cinder path, sir.

—Hoho! The cinder path!, cried the prefect of studies. I know that trick.

Stephen lifted his eyes in wonder and saw for a moment Father Dolan's whitegrey not young face, his baldy whitegrey head with fluff at the sides of it, the steel rims of his spectacles and his nocoloured eyes looking through the glasses. Why did he say he knew that trick?

—Lazy, idle little loafer!, cried the prefect of studies. Broke my glasses! An old schoolboy trick! Out with your hand this moment!

Stephen closed his eyes and held out in the air his trembling hand with the palm upwards. He felt the prefect of studies touch it for a moment at the fingers to straighten it and then the swish of the sleeve of the soutane as the pandybat was lifted to strike. A hot burning stinging tingling blow like the loud crack of a broken stick made his trembling hand crumple together like a leaf in the fire: and at the sound and the pain scalding tears were driven into his eyes. His whole body was shaking with fright, his arm was shaking and his crumpled burning livid hand shook like a loose leaf in the air. A cry sprang to his lips, a prayer to be let off. But though the tears scalded his eyes and his limbs quivered with pain and fright he held back the hot tears and the cry that scalded his throat.

—Other hand! shouted the prefect of studies.

Stephen drew back his maimed and quivering right arm and held out his left hand. The soutane sleeve swished again as the pandybat was lifted and a loud crashing sound and a fierce maddening tingling burning pain made his hand shrink together with the palm and fingers in a livid quivering mass. The scalding water burst forth from his eyes and burning with shame and agony and fear, he drew back his shaking arm in terror and burst out into a whine of pain. His body shook with a palsy of fright and in shame and rage he felt the scalding cry come from his throat and the scalding tears falling out of his eyes and down his flaming cheeks.

— Kneel down! cried the prefect of studies.

Stephen knelt down, quickly pressing his beaten hands to his sides. To think of them beaten and swollen with pain all in a moment made him so sorry for them as if they were not his own but someone else's that he felt sorry for. And as he knelt, calming the last sobs in his throat and feeling the burning tingling pain pressed into his sides, he thought of the hands which he had held out in the air with the palms up and of the firm touch of the prefect of studies when he had steadied his shaking fingers and of the beaten swollen reddened mass of palm and fingers that shook helplessly in the air.

— Get at your work, all of you, cried the prefect of studies from the door. Father Dolan will be in every day to see if any boy, any lazy idling little loafer wants flogging. Every day. Every day.

The door closed behind him.

The injustice of the punishment leads young Stephen to go to the Rector (the principal) of the school. This daring reveals early in the novel Stephen's strength of character and independence. He wants to complain about the injustice of his punishment. The Rector listens to Stephen, perhaps with some amusement, tells Stephen he'll think about it and take care of it, and then sends him away. For Joyce this event in his growing up was one that he remembered, and it helped in shaping some of his negative attitudes, towards the Church and its justice.

Another significant incident occurs when Stephen goes home for Christmas holidays. A political dispute develops at the Christmas table about Parnell, who has just been unseated as a result of the scandal. The discussion of Parnell turns to the Church's involvement in Irish politics. You will recall that when the Church withdrew its support from Parnell, it insured that the National League would unseat him as chairman. Yet Parnell had been the most forceful advocate for home rule for Ireland. At the Christmas table one family member criticizes the Church's action, whereupon others rise up in vigorous defense of anything the Church chooses to do. The young boy sits quietly, quite startled and impressed by the heated discussion.

— And am I to sit hear and listen to the pastors of my Church being flouted?

—Nobody is saying a word against them, said Mr. Dedalus, so long as they don't meddle in politics.

—The bishops and the priests of Ireland have spoken, said Dante, and they must be obeyed.

—Let them leave politics alone, said Mr. Casey, or the people may leave their Church alone.

—You hear? said Dante turning to Mrs. Dedalus.

—Mr. Casey! Simon! said Mrs. Dedalus. Let it end now.

—Too bad! Too bad! said uncle Charles.

—What? cried Mr. Dedalus. Were we to desert him at the bidding of the English people?

—He was no longer worthy to lead said Dante. He was a public sinner.

—We're all sinners and black sinners, said Mr. Casey coldly.

— *Woe to the man by whom the scandal cometh*, said Mrs. Riordan. *It would be better for him that a millstone were tied about his neck and that he were cast into the depth of the sea rather than that he should scandalise one of these, my least little ones.* That is the language of the Holy Ghost.

—And very bad language if you ask me said Mr. Dedalus. Coolly. . . .

—Really, Simon, said Mrs. Dedalus, you should not speak that way before Stephen. It's not right.

—O, he'll remember all this when he grows up, said Dante hotly—The language he heard against God and against religion and priests in his own home.

—Let him remember, too, cried Mr. Casey to her from across the table, the language with which the priests and the priest's pawns broke Parnell's heart and hounded him into his grave. Let him remember that too when he grows up.

—Sons o' bitches! cried Mr. Dedalus. When he was down they turned to him to betray him and rend him like rats in a sewer. Lowlived dogs! And they took it! By Christ they took it!

—They behaved rightly cried Dante. They obeyed their bishops and their priests. Honour to them.

—Well, it's perfectly dreadful to say that not even for one day in the year, said Mrs. Dedalus, can we be free from these dreadful disputes!

And of course Stephen does discover and remember Parnell, and he does ponder the interrelationship of politics and religion in Ireland throughout the rest of the book. Recollections about Parnell recur throughout the novel. And Joyce's recollections and his own experience and knowledge of the unseating of Parnell are there for him to use in making mature assessments about his country and in deciding to leave it.

In some of the most memorable and effective sections of the book, Joyce stuns the reader with sermons that Stephen hears on a religious retreat at school. Although too long to quote at length, they deserve examination, for they are some of the best parts of the book. They also represent a style of sermonizing familiar, at least in years past, to children throughout Ireland.

The sermons emphasize the agonies of hell; they detail its fire and brimstone. First, a long section deals with the darkness of hell. Next discussion shifts to the stench of hell. Then the preacher describes the continual physical torment of burning in the fires of hell. Especially emphasized is the excruciating and endless intensity of spiritual torment caused by deprivation—the pain of the loss of the presence of God, the pain of the person's conscience in hell for all eternity.

The paragraphs on eternity are especially intriguing and effective. These passages, as Keats would say, "tease us out of thought," because the finite mind and the physical body in the world of time cannot conceive of the nature of infinity, the endlessness of something without a beginning and without an end. The priest gives careful attention to the nature of eternity and the endlessness of the physical pain of hell. His effectiveness depends upon his analogies.

> Last and crowning torture of all of the tortures of that awful place is the eternity of hell. Eternity! O dread and dire word. Eternity! What mind of man can understand it? And, remember, it is an eternity of pain. Even though the pains of hell were not so terrible as they are yet they would become infinite as they are destined to last forever. But while they are everlasting they are at the same time, as you know, intolerably intense, unbearable extensive. To bear even the sting of an insect for eternity would be a dreadful torment. What must it be, then, to bear the manifold tortures of hell for ever? For ever! For all eternity! Not for a year or for an age but forever. Try to imagine the awful meaning of this. You have often seen the sand on the seashore. How fine are its tiny grains! And how many of those tiny little grains go to make up the small handful which a child grasps in its play. Now imagine a mountain of that sand, a million miles high, reaching from the earth to the farthest heavens, and a million miles broad, extending to the

remotest space, and a million miles in thickness: and imagine such an enormous mass of countless particles of sand multiplied as often as there are leaves in the forest, drops of water in the mighty ocean, feathers on birds, scales on fish, hairs on animals, atoms in the vast expanse of the air: and imagine at the end of every million years a little bird came to that mountain and carried away in its beak a tiny grain of that sand. How many millions upon millions of centuries would pass before that bird had carried away every square foot of that mountain, how many eons upon eons of ages before it had carried away all? Yet at the end of that immense stretch of time not even one instant of eternity could be said to have ended. At the end of all those billions and trillions of years eternity would have scarcely begun. And if that mountain rose again after it had been all carried away and the bird came again and carried it all away again grain by grain: and if it so rose and sank as many times as there are stars in the sky, atoms in the air, drops of water in the sea, leaves on the trees, feathers upon the birds, scales upon the fish, hairs upon the animals, at the end of all those innumerable risings and sinkings of that immeasurably vast mountain not one single instant of eternity could be said to have ended; even then, at the end of such a period, after that eon of time the mere thought of which makes our very brain reel dizzily, eternity would have scarcely begun.

The sermons on hell and its eternal torments have an overwhelming effect on Stephen. He thinks they are meant specifically for him in his sinful state, so in guilt and agony he goes to confess his sins and struggles desperately to devote himself to God as the Church indicates. Since inherent in the religious upbringing of the Irish boy is the implication that a man's highest calling is to the priesthood, Stephen debates at great length whether he should take religious vows.

His adolescence has brought about normal sexual urgings and experimentations, and Stephen wallows in excruciating guilt for each of his acts. His guilt is confirmed by the teachings of the Church. A similar guilt is painfully narrated in John McGahern's recent novel *The Dark*. In *Portrait*, though Stephen struggles against himself, he is still drawn to the neighborhood of brothels. Young Stephen is almost magnetized to that part of town, partially out of curiosity. So begins one of the major conflicts in the novel, that between the flesh and the spirit. Stephen's soul has been directed by his Church to ways antithetical to the drive of his senses. Seemingly he cannot serve them both. His nightime forays in Dublin contain all the fearful attractiveness of adolescence:

> He had wandered into a maze of narrow and dirty streets. From the foul laneways he heard bursts of hoarse laughter and wrangling and the drawling of drunken singers. . . . Women and girls dressed in long, vivid gowns, traversed the streets from house to house. They were leisurely and perfumed. A trembling seized him and his eyes grew dim. The yellow gas flames arose before his troubled vision against the vapoury skies, burning as if before an altar. Before the doors and in the lighted halls groups were gathered arrayed as for some rite. He was in another world: he had awakened from a slumber of centuries.
>
> He stood still in the middle of the roadway, his heart clamouring against his bosom in a tumult. A young woman dressed in a long pink gown laid her hands on his arm to detain him and gazed into his face. She said gaily
> —Good night, Willie dear!
>
> Her room was warm and lightsome. . . . He tried to bid his tongue speak that he might seem at ease, watching her as she undid her gown, noting the proud conscious movements of her perfumed head.
>
> As he stood silent in the middle of the room she came over to him and embraced him gaily and gravely. Her round arms held him firmly to her and he, seeing her face lifted to him in serious calm and feeling the warm calm rise and fall of her breast, all but burst into hysterical weeping. Tears of joy and relief shown in his delighted eyes and his lips parted though they would not speak.
>
> She passed her tinkling hand through his hair, calling him a little rascal.
> —Give me a kiss, she said.
>
> His lips would not bend to kiss her. He wanted to be held firmly in her arms, to be caressed slowly, slowly, slowly. In her arms he felt that he had suddenly become strong and fearless and sure of himself. But his lips would not bend to kiss her.
>
> With a sudden movement she bowed his head and joined her lips to his and he read the meaning of her movements in her frank uplifted eyes. It was too much for him. He closed his eyes, surrendering himself to her, body and mind, conscious of nothing in the world but the dark pressure of her softly parting lips. They pressed upon his brain as upon his lips as though they were the vehicle of a vague speech; and between them he felt an unknown

and timid pressure, darker than the swoon of sin, softer than sound
or odour.

For Stephen, however, waves of tormenting guilt follow this particular experience in growing up. His conscience wars with his flesh.

Stephen also experiences great pain when he feels he has grown
beyond his family. He feels that they're too common. All to frequently they blast his interior ideal. Any number of times as Stephen
fantacizes idealistic goals and expectations, the realities of family
and daily life intrude. His parents make mockery of his yearnings,
and he comes to think that he knows and feels things his family can
never understand. One passage will illustrate this point. Stephen has
just crossed the bridge over a stream.

> [He] turned his eyes coldly for an instant towards the faded blue
> shrine of the Blessed Virgin which stood fowlwise on a pole in the
> middle of a ham-shaped encampment of poor cottages. Then,
> bending to the left, he followed the lane which led up to his house.
> The faint sour stink of rotted cabbages came towards him from the
> kitchengardens on the rising ground above the river. He smiled to
> think that it was this disorder, the misrule and confusion of his
> father's house and the stagnation of vegetable life, which was to
> win the day in his soul. Then a short laugh broke his lips.

In the immediate contrast between Stephen's viewing the statue of
the Virgin and then the intrusion of the stink of rotted cabbage in
his father's garden, we can see the kind of disenchantment and
disgust that Stephen feels for his own household.

Thus, Stephen feels he is being suppressed or held down by his
own family, by his Church, by his country, held down by these three
nets, as he calls them. He thinks the development of his own in-
dividuality and his own soul is being thwarted. But just as he was independent and strong when he went to the Rector of the school to
complain about the injustice of his beating, so as the book reaches
its conclusion Stephen exercises the same kind of strength and independence when he decides to escape, to leave Ireland, to fly
beyond the confining nets. Throughout Stephen's growing up he
continually nurtured his own interior ideals, his own yearnings after
a kind of perfection; they give him a dedication that we can see in
this representative passage:

> Sometimes a fever gathered within him and led him to rove alone

in the evening along the quiet avenue. The peace of the gardens and the kindly lights in the windows poured a tender influence into his restless heart. The noise of children at play annoyed him and their silly voices made him feel, even more keenly than he had felt at Clongowes, that he was different from others. He did not want to play. He wanted to meet in the real world the unsubstantial image which his soul so constantly beheld. He did not know where to seek it or how: but a premonition which led him on told him that this image would, without any overt act of his, encounter him. They would meet quietly as if they had known each other and had made their tryst, perhaps at one of the gates or in some more secret place. They would be alone, surrounded by darkness and silence: and in that moment of supreme tenderness he would be transfigured. He would fade into something impalpable under her eyes and then in a moment, he would be transfigured. Weakness and timidity and inexperience would fall from him in that magic moment.

At a critical moment in the book, then, Stephen comes to a decision as a result of the discoveries he has been making. Weakness and timidity fall from him in his magic momet: he will not serve his Church or his country. He uses the Latin terms — *non serviam* — I will not serve. His dedication is "to discover the mode of life or of art whereby his spirit could express itself in unfettered freedom." Stephen will free himself from home, from fatherland, and from the Church. His ideals and his interest in art — in writing — lead him to his new dedication. He decides that "he would create proudly out of the freedom and power of his own soul, as the great artificer whose name he bore, a living thing, new and soaring and beautiful, impalpable, imperishable." By the end of the book, a mature Stephen, much like Joyce, goes forth "to encounter for the millionth time the reality of experience and to forge in the smithy of my soul the uncreated conscience of my race."

Thus, for Joyce the experiences of growing up really hurt his book into existence. Joyce left Ireland, but Ireland remained his subject matter until his death. He didn't really escape as he had hoped, but he exercised his artistic power over Ireland as he recreated it in the art of his writing. The conclusion to *A Portrait of the Artist as a Young Man*, the forging in the smithy of his soul, the expression of the conscience of his race, as Joyce says, recalls the end of Yeats' "Sailing to Byzantium," in which Yeats wants to find spiritual permanence in his art, symbolically represented by the

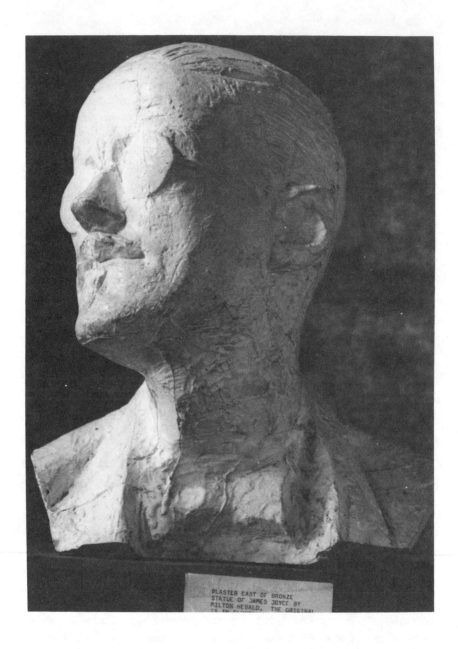

31. A plaster cast of the bust of James Joyce over his grave. The bust calls attention
to Joyce's lifetime difficulty with his eyesight. (Irish Tourist Board)

32. John McGahern, the contemporary fiction writer. (©Jim Kalett)

golden bird on the golden trees singing of what is past, passing, and
to come. For Joyce, the forging of his own soul and the expression of
it in *A Portrait of the Artist as a Young Man* hardens into the permanence of art his own experiences of childhood and maturation.

The novel *The Dark*, by John McGahern, published in 1965,
treats of growing up more recently in Ireland. McGahern himself
was born in 1935; he spent his childhood in the West of Ireland. The
repressive forces in *The Dark* recall those of Joyce, but *The Dark*
also contains a newer sort of defeat at its conclusion. The opening
scene of the novel immediately reminds the reader of Joyce, most
particularly of the punishment meted out to Stephen for breaking
his glasses. But in *The Dark* it's the young boys' outraged widower

father who administers the punishment. The scene is a compelling illustration of the strength of McGahern's prose as well as a frightening picture of parental tyranny.

"Say what you said because I know."

"I didn't say anything."

"Out with it I tell you."

"I don't know I said anything."

"F-U-C-K is what you said, isn't it? That profane and ugly word. Now do you think you can bluff your way out of it?"

"I didn't mean, it just came out!"

"The filth that's in your head came out, you mean. And I'm going to teach you a lesson for once. You'd think there'd be some respect for your dead mother left in the house. And trying to sing dumb — as if butter wouldn't melt. But I'll teach you."

He took the heavy leather strap he used for sharpening his razor from its nail on the side of the press.

"Come on with me. Upstairs. I'll teach you a lesson for once. I'll teach you a lesson for once," he said with horrible measured passion through his teeth, the blood mounted to his face. "I'll teach you a lesson this house won't forget in a hurry."

"I didn't mean it, Daddy. I didn't mean it, it just slipped out."

"Up the stairs. March. I'm telling you. Up the stairs."

By the shoulder Mahoney pushed him out the door into the hallway towards the stairs.

"March, march, march," he kept grinding as they went. "Quickly. No, not in there," when he turned for the room where they both slept together. "Into the girls' room. This'll have to be witnessed. I'll teach a lesson this house won't forget."

The two large beds where all the girls slept faced the door, the little table between them, and above it on the wall the picture of the Ascension. A plywood wardrobe and a black leather armchair stood beside the empty fireplace. Mona rose out of the bedclothes in fright at their coming.

"I'm going to teach this gent a lesson. Your sister can be witness of this. Now off with your clothes. I'm going to teach you a lesson. Quick. Strip. Off with your clothes."

Slowly, in a dazed horror, he got off his jacket and wept.

"No. I didn't mean it, Daddy. It just slipped out."

"Off with your jersey. Quick. We can't stand here all day," a white froth showed on his lips. The eyes stared out beyond the walls of the room. The belt twitched against his trousers, an animal's tail.

"Off with the trousers. Off with trousers."

"No, no."

"Off with the trousers, I said."

He just moved closer. He didn't lift a hand, as if the stripping compelled by his will alone gave him pleasure.

"Off with the trousers," and with frightened weeping the trousers were let slip down around the ankles on the floor.

"Off with the shirt," he ground quietly, and when the shirt was off the boy stood completely naked. With the belt he pointed to the armchair.

"Into that chair with you. On your mouth and nose. I'll give your arse something it won't forget in a hurry."

"No, Daddy, no. I didn't mean," he gave one last whimper but he had to lie in the chair, lie there and wait as a broken animal. Something in him snapped. He couldn't control his water and it flowed from him over the leather of the seat. He'd never imagined horror such as this, waiting naked for the leather to come down on his flesh, would it ever come, it was impossible and yet nothing could be much worse than this waiting.

"I'll teach you a lesson for once," and then he cried out as the leather came, exploding with a shot on the leather of the armrest over his ear, his whole body stiff, sweat breaking, and it was impossible to realize he hadn't actually been hit yet.

"No, no, no," he cried as he tried to rise.

"Don't move. Don't move. Move and I'll cut that arse off you. I'm only giving you a taste of what you're going to get. I'm just showing you and shut that shouting," and he was willed by fear back on his mouth and nose, not able to move, shivering fits beginning to come, and the anguish and squalor was impossible, but would the black leather cut across his flesh this time, it was horrible and worse than death to think.

It came as it came before, a rifle crack on the armrest, the same hysterical struggle, and he hadn't been hit yet, it was unreal.

"Don't move and shut that shouting," and when he was reasonably still except for the shivering and weeping, the leather came for the third time exactly as before. He didn't know anything or what he was doing or where the room was when the leather exploded on the black armrest beside where his ear was.

"Shut up that racket and get on your feet. Quick. And shut up. It's on the bare skin you'll get it the next time but that taste'll do for this time. Get your clothes on you. You can count yourself lucky. Get up. Get up."

It was such a struggle to realize it was over. He had to try to get on his feet out of the chair, it was a kind of tearing, and to stand naked on the floor. The shivering fits of crying came and went, but quieter. He was only aware of Mona's frightened wailing in the bed when Mahoney shouted, "You in the bed shut up before you get cause. Shut up now. Let that be a lesson to you. I don't know whether it's sick you are or foxing in that bed these last days. And you — you get your clothes, and waste no time getting downstairs," he turned to the naked boy before he left the room, his face still red and heated, the leather hanging dead in his hand.

It was a real struggle to get each piece of clothing on after he'd gone, the hands clumsy and shaking. The worst was the vapoury rush of thoughts, he couldn't get any grip on what had happened to him, he'd never known such a pit of horror as he'd touched, nothing seemed to matter any more. His mother had gone away years before and left him to this. Day of sunshine he'd picked wild strawberries for her on the railway she was dying.

"Did he hit you at all?" Mona was asking from the bed.

"No."

The word opened such a floodgate that he had to hurry out of the room with the last of his clothes in his hands, by the front door out to the old bolted refuge of the lavatory, with the breeze blowing in its one airhole. There they all rushed hours as these to sit in the comforting darkness and reek of Jeyes Fluid to weep and grope their way in hatred and selfpity to some sort of calm.

In the novel, which in large measure treats of the son's relationship with his father as the son grows up, the boy is troubled with sex and religion, again somewhat reminiscent of Joyce. The book faces explicitly the boy's habitual masturbation, caused in large measure, it is suggested, by the pressures and restrictions laid on to him. His masturbation leads to devastating bouts of guilt, and the book is effectively moving in tracing these troubling introspective journeys. Much of the boy's guilt is generated by the Church's rigidity in defining and dealing with the "impurity" of masturbation. For the boy his sins of impurity stand seriously in the way of his considerations about becoming a priest. Since the boy is intelligent and successful in school, he is urged, somewhat typically for Ireland, into declaring a vocation. The boy brings his conflicts to a priest, who himself bears scars of sexual frustration as well as physical illness. After the boy nervously prepares and sits for a university scholarship examination, he wins the scholarship and sees the university as an escape from home and a way to an education apart from the

33. The entire student body and their teacher in the school yard of their school in County Mayo.

priesthood. But the university opens up a fearful new life, and a lonely one; his earlier years have not prepared him for its emotional demands. He hasn't escaped himself and his own inner turmoil, which the novel continues to chart effectively and touchingly. Near the end of the book, he is unjustly expelled from a physics classroom when the teacher, in an apparently regular display of power, accuses him incorrectly of "hooliganism." McGahern presents the boy's response, as he considers leaving the university:

> You went down the tarmacadam, Brady's cursed class in progress to your right, out under the drips of the green oaks along University Road. The tar shone in the rain. The town faced you, smoke mixed in the rain above the houses. You'd to make up your mind. Either to go and apologize to Brady and face three years cramming here or go to Dublin to the job. It wasn't Brady drove you, you'd go and crawl for him if it was worth it, only a fool stood up, you could go and crawl and savage him after you got the chance and wanted still. But maybe it was the fall of the dice, you were meant to go, and if anything happened here there was no one to turn to,

not Mahoney [his father]. It was better to go and it'd be better to
do it at once and tell Mahoney.

In the post office near Moon's Corner you wasted several
telegram forms till you were satisfied with,

WANT TO TAKE E.S.B. AND LEAVE UNI.,

WILL WAIT FOR YOUR CONSENT.

They said at the counter that he'd have it in about two hours.

Thus the boy collapses and retreats depressingly to a clerk's job
with the E.S.B., the Electricity Supply Board, in Dublin. His
reasons are clear in his subsequent conversations:

"The course is too long," he says to his father. . . . "With the
E.S.B., I'd be earning money straight away," you'd learned long
ago the kind of reasons to present, no use giving your own reasons,
but reasons closest to where it touched Mahoney." Mahoney asks
him to get guidance in his decision from a priest at the university.
To him the boy says,

"I'm afraid I might get sick or fail and there's more in the house
besides me, father," and it sounded as lame as it was.

"You're afraid of failing?"

"I am father."

"You'd not have to worry about that in the E.S.B.," the priest
looked you straight in the face and you saw what he was doing and
hated him for it. The Dean was forcing you to decide for yourself.

"No. I'd not have to worry."

"Well, I definitely think you should take the E.S.B. so," there
seemed contempt in his voice, you and Mahoney would never give
commands but be always menials to the race he'd come from and
still belonged to, you'd make a schoolteacher at best. You might
have your uses but you were both his stableboys, and would never
eat at his table.

It was hard to walk quiet out of the University at Mahoney's side
and see the goalposts luminous in the grey light of the rain and not
give savage expression to one murderous feeling of defeat.

But it is defeat, and the novel closes with it. The intelligent and
sensitive boy's difficult and painful growing up has led, not to
Stephen's affirmative declaration of independence, but to a lifetime
in a nondescript and boring job as a clerk with the E.S.B. He
becomes, in a sense, a potential character in the cast of Joyce's
Dubliners. The various repressions that he had struggled against in

his growing up have won out and have closed in around the young man and have taken him in. It is the culminating depression of the book, a book which has compellingly presented the solitude and interior life of this growing boy. McGahern's strength arises out of his ultimate theme, that while perhaps not lonely, everyone is alone in the world, in his own world, in solitude. To grow up in Ireland is to grow up into this isolation and solitude.

Conclusion

THE LITERATURE of Ireland goes on; what we have briefly ex-
amined is not a story which ends or which I can tidily sum
up as having taken some final shape. I did not begin to
mention all matters of importance in Irish literature, but rather I
hope to have tempted readers to seek out more about this lovely land
and its fine writing on their own. The literature of Ireland has been
a nationally introspective one, self-consciously taking as its subject
matter its own political and social life, its own troubled past and
present history. Irish national feeling and the assertion of a national
soul have fired Irish literature and ignited Ireland's national
rebellions. These rebellions have then, in an ever-dynamic cycle,
generated more drama, more fiction, more poetry and song. Irish
literature has struggled to capture the wildly imaginative life of the
countryside—that product of a primitive people isolated and
desperately impoverished in a landscape of incomparable, and
unspoiled, beauty. And it has etched, with fine precision, the often
meager and limiting realities of Dublin city life. Irish literature has
looked deep into the individual too, dissecting the shaping years of
childhood and laying bare the dreams, ideals, and psychological
pain of adulthood. How palpably the people of Ireland live in their
literature!

Such turning inward, such introspective penetration, both of
the nation and of individuals, has not, paradoxically, limited the attraction that the literature of this small and remote island has for

readers everywhere. Irish writers have depicted the life and people of Ireland within a universe that includes such grand spiritual and abstract forces, such vast nihilistic desolation and emptiness, that Irish literature takes its place among all the world's great literatures. Although Irish literature turns in on itself, it also expands into a universal immensity. Its writers in the twentieth century stand at the foundation of the century's great literature, and presentation of life in Ireland has become a presentation of life itself.

Suggestions For Further Reading

As a supplement to the works and authors discussed in the text of the book, I present this highly selective and by no means comprehensive list of suggested readings.

Beckett, Samuel. The many prose and dramatic works of this Irish-born writer who now lives in France are sometimes enigmatic, sometimes comic, and always depressing. His outstanding play is *Waiting for Godot*; notable novels include *Malone Dies, Molloy,* and *Murphy.*

Behan, Brendan. Major plays by this popular dramatist are *The Hostage* and *The Quare Fellow. Borstal Boy* is Behan's lively autobiographical narrative.

Brown, Malcolm. *The Politics of Irish Literature from Thomas Davis to W.B. Yeats.* London, 1972. Interweavings of politics and literature in the latter half of the nineteen century.

Brown, Terence. *Ireland: A Social and Cultural History, 1922–79.* London, 1981. A discussion of life in Ireland in recent times.

Caulfield, Max. *The Easter Rebellion.* London, 1964. The details of the insurrection of 1916.

Dangerfield, George. *The Damnable Question.* Boston, 1976. An authorative, interestingly written analysis of the Anglo-Irish conflict.

Devlin, Bernadette. *The Price of My Soul.* London, 1969. Her youth and upbringing in Northern Ireland, as told by the political activist and civil rights leader.

Dillon, Myles and Nora Chadwick. *The Celtic Realms.* London, 1976. General attention to Celtic life.

The Earl of Longford and Thomas P. O'Neill. *Eamon de Valera.* London, 1970. The authorized biography of the modern military and political figure.

Ellis-Fermor, Una. *The Irish Dramatic Movement.* London, 1939. The development of Irish theater.

Ellmann, Richard. *James Joyce.* New York, 1959. The full and richly detailed biography of this major writer.

Encyclopedia of Ireland. Dublin and New York, 1968. A useful general reference, divided into broad range of sections comprehensively dealing with aspects of Ireland. Illustrated.

Fallis, Richard. *The Irish Renaissance.* Syracuse, N.Y., 1977. A discussion of the literary movement in Ireland in modern times.

Farrell, Michael. *Thy Tears Might Cease.* New York, 1964. A moving novel of growing up in the violence and chaos of Ireland from 1910 to 1920.

Friel, Brian. The contemporary playwright and fiction writer whose play *Philadelphia, Here I Come* dramatizes with humor and interior penetration the departure of an emigrant. The play *Translations* dramatizes the change in culture brought about in Ireland by the institution of primary education in 1831.

Greene, David H. *Irish Literature.* New York, 1971. A two-volume anthology of selected pieces of literature from twelve hundred years of writings.

Gregory, Lady Isabella Augusta. A friend of W.B. Yeats, Lady Gregory collected and retold ancient myths and stories of Ireland in *Visions and Beliefs in the West of Ireland, Cuchulain of Muirthemne: The Story of the Man of the Red Branch of Ulster,* and *Gods and Fighting Men: The Story of the Tuatha DeNanaan and the Fianna of Ireland.* She is also notable for her one-act plays, most particularly "The Rising of the Moon," about the hiding of an insurrectionist, and "Spreading the News, a comedy about small-town gossip.

Guide to the National Monuments in the Republic of Ireland. Dublin, 1970. Practical and informational reference guide.

Guiness, Desmond and William Ryan. *Irish Houses and Castles.* London, 1971. A book with beautiful interior and exterior photographs of big houses of the Georgian period in Ireland, published by the Irish Georgian Society.

Heaney, Seumas. A fine contemporary poet of firm ability. His works include *Wintering Out, North,* and, most recently, *Fieldwork.*

Hoagland, Kathleen, ed. *1000 Years of Irish Poetry.* New York, 1947. Representative poems from pagan times to the present.

Ireland Yesterday, introduction by Maurice Gorham. New York, 1971. A collection of old photographs depicting aspects of life in Ireland.

Joyce, James. In addition to *Dubliners* and *A Portrait of the Artist as a Young Man*, which are discussed in this book, Joyce is also known for his famous and complex *Ulysses* and his forbiddingly difficult *Finnegan's Wake.*

Kiely, Benedict. Among the many entertaining short stories told by Kiely are those in *Journey to Seven Streams* and in *The State of*

Ireland. His *Proxopera* is a short and stark novel of conflict in Northern Ireland.

Kinsella, Thomas. A leading contemporary poet from Ireland, notable for his translation of the ancient Irish epic *The Tain.*

Lavin, Mary. A prolific contemporary short-story writer of penetrating humanity. Almost any story of hers can become a favorite.

Leonard, Hugh. The contemporary playwright whose play "Da" presents with humor and growing affectionate understanding the maturing process with humor and humanity. *Home Before Night* is Leonard's biographical prose recreation of his own Dublin childhood.

Lyons, F.S.L. *Ireland Since the Famine.* London, 1971. The most authorative and complete history of the period since the mid-1800s.

———. *Charles Stewart Parnell.* New York, 1977. The full and authorative biography of the political leader.

MacCana, Proinsias. *Celtic Mythology.* The Celtic myths, stories, gods, and goddesses.

Macken, Walter. This popular writer is best known for his historical trilogy of life in Ireland in the nineteenth century, *The Fair Land, The Silent People,* and *The Scorching Wind.* Also a writer of plays and short stories.

MacLaverty, Bernard. A contemporary fiction writer who has been highly praised for *Cal* (New York, 1983), his novel of the inner and outer turmoil of life in present-day Northern Ireland.

Mercier, Vivian and David H. Greene, eds. *1000 Years of Irish Prose.* New York, 1952. Well-selected pieces of representative prose from the literary revival.

Moody, T.W. and F.X. Martin, eds. Cork, 1967. *The Course of Irish History.* A very readable history of Ireland.

Moore, Brian. Moore now lives in the United States. His early novel *The Lonely Passion of Judith Hearne* is a compassionate novel of loneliness in Belfast.

O'Brien, Conor Cruise, ed. *The Shaping of Modern Ireland.* London, 1960. An interesting survey of people and currents shaping modern Ireland.

O'Casey, Sean. In addition to O'Casey's play "The Plough and the Stars" discussed in this book, are his plays "Juno and the Paycock," "The Shadow of a Gunman," "The Silver Tassie," and "Red Roses for Me." His autobiographies, including *I Knock at the Door, Pictures in the Hallway, Drums Under the Windows* tell of his development from his impoverished Dublin youth.

O'Connor, Frank. Among the famous short stories of this popular and prolific writer are "Guests of the Nation," "The Train," "Uprooted,"

"Judas," "My Oedipus Complex," "Custom of the Country," "The Bridal Night."

O'Faolain, Sean. *King of the Beggars.* A life of Daniel O'Connell by the contemporary short-story writer.

————. A wide-ranging and sophisticated master of the short story whose work spans several decades. Among his many superior stories are "Admiring the Scenery," "Broken World," "Lovers of the Lake," "Silence of the Valley," "Foreign Affairs." O'Faolain's autobiography, *Vive Moi* is written with interest and zest.

O'Flaherty, Liam. O'Flaherty's novel *The Informer* is probably his best-known work in the United States because it was made into a notable film. His other novel of note is *Famine.* In addition to "Going Into Exile," his short story discussed in the book, other fine stories are "Spring Sowing," "The Lovely Beasts," "His First Flight."

Orel, Harold. *Irish History and Culture.* Lawrence, Kansas, 1976. A collection of essays tracing the cultural history of Ireland.

Plunkett, James. The sequel to *Strumpet City,* discussed in this book, is *Farewell Companions,* which focuses on the years from 1914 to 1918 in Ireland and is not as effectively told.

Pritchett, V.S. *Dublin: A Portrait.* New York, 1967. A beautifully written depiction of Dublin, with stunning photographs by Evelyn Hofer.

Synge, John Millington. In addition to Synge's plays, "Riders to the Sea" and "The Playboy of the Western World," discussed in this book, there are four others: "In the Shadow of the Glen," "The Tinker's Wedding," "The Well of Saints," "Deirdre of the Sorrows." *"The Aran Islands"* is Synge's interesting account of his time on the Aran Islands and his observations on daily life there.

Thompson, William I. *The Imagination of an Insurrection: Dublin, Easter 1916.* New York, 1967. An interesting interweaving of literature and the 1916 insurrection.

Unterecker, John. *A Reader's Guide to William Butler Yeats.* New York, 1959. A helpful guide and interpretation to individual poems of Yeats.

Woodham-Smith, Cecil. *The Great Hunger.* London, 1962. An authentic and gripping history of the potato famine of the mid-nineteenth century.

Yeats, William Butler. Yeats' work is so varied and superior that it is impossible not to overlook fine works when suggesting other poems for reading in addition to the poems and play discussed in this book. John Unterecker's *A Reader's Guide to William Butler Yeats* is suggested for use with *The Collected Poems of W.B. Yeats* (New York,

1956). Among the poems no one should overlook are: "When You Are Old," "The Cap and Bells," "He Wishes His Beloved Were Dead," "The Song of the Old Mother," "He Reproves the Curfew," "Adam's Curse," "The Magic," "The Wild Swans at Coole," "An Irish Airman Forsees His Death," "The Second Coming," "Leda and the Swan," "Byzantium," "I am of Ireland," "The Statues," "The Long-Legged Fly," "Under Ben Bulben,"

Index